IMPROVING THE
RELATIONAL SPACE OF
CURRICULUM REALISATION

EMERALD PROFESSIONAL LEARNING NETWORK SERIES

Series Editors: Chris Brown, University of Portsmouth, UK and Cindy Poortman, University of Twente, The Netherlands

In the current international policy environment, teachers are viewed as learning-oriented adaptive experts. Required to be able to teach increasingly diverse sets of learners, teachers must be competent in complex academic content, skilful in the craft of teaching and able to respond to fast changing economic and policy imperatives. The knowledge, skills and attitudes needed for this complex profession requires teachers to engage in collaborative and networked career-long learning. The types of learning networks emerging to meet this need comprise a variety of collaborative arrangements including inter-school engagement, as well as collaborations with learning partners, such as universities or policy-makers. More understanding is required, however, on how learning networks can deliver maximum benefit for both teachers and students.

Emerald Professional Learning Network Series aims to expand current understanding of professional learning networks and the impact of harnessing effective networked collaboration.

IMPROVING THE RELATIONAL SPACE OF CURRICULUM REALISATION: SOCIAL NETWORK INTERVENTIONS

BY

CLAIRE SINNEMA
The University of Auckland, New Zealand

ALAN J. DALY
University of California, USA

JOELLE RODWAY
Memorial University of Newfoundland, Canada

DARREN HANNAH
The University of Auckland, New Zealand

RACHEL CANN
The University of Auckland, New Zealand

AND

YI-HWA LIOU
National Taipei University of Education, Taiwan

emerald
PUBLISHING

United Kingdom – North America – Japan – India
Malaysia – China

Emerald Publishing Limited
Howard House, Wagon Lane, Bingley BD16 1WA, UK

First edition 2023

Reprints and permissions service
Contact: www.copyright.com

British Library Cataloguing in Publication Data
A catalogue record for this book is available from the British Library

ISBN: 978-1-80382-516-8 (Print)
ISBN: 978-1-80382-513-7 (Online)
ISBN: 978-1-80382-515-1 (Epub)

Printed and bound by CPI Group (UK) Ltd, Croydon, CR0 4YY

CONTENTS

LIST OF FIGURES AND TABLES

Figures

Tables

ABOUT THE AUTHORS

Claire Sinnema is an Associate Professor at The University of Auckland. Her research deals with educational improvement and the realisation of curriculum and other educational policies in practice. Her work addresses the role of curriculum design, networks, practitioner inquiry, leadership and problem-solving in educational contexts.

Alan J. Daly is a Professor and the Director of Educational Leadership Doctoral Programs in the Department of Education Studies at the University of California, San Diego. His research primarily focusses on the role of social networks and their impacts on social systems.

Joelle Rodway is an Assistant Professor at the Memorial University of Newfoundland. Her research is on the role of social capital in whole system educational change.

Darren Hannah is an EdD graduate of The University of Auckland. His research interest is the generation of actionable knowledge that can be used for organisational improvement through the diagnosis of and engagement with theories of action.

Rachel Cann is a PhD candidate at the University of Auckland. Her research relates to the individual, relational and organizational influences on educator wellbeing, drawing on positive psychology and social network theory.

Yi-Hwa Liou, Professor of the Department of Educational Management at the National Taipei University of Education, Taiwan. She researches leadership and development and professional and networked learning communities using social network analysis.

ACKNOWLEDGEMENTS

This book is both *about* collaboration and arises *from* collaboration. We would like to acknowledge the new relational ties that were established between our project team, and the many teachers and curriculum leaders in schools and across the two communities of learning that we worked in. The design of our project was co-constructed with many of them, and we greatly value their commitment to and energy for the work! We have enormous respect for their receptiveness to new ways of thinking about their leadership practice, and their efforts to foreground the relational space in support of curriculum realisation.

ACKNOWLEDGMENTS

INTRODUCTION

In this book, we offer insights into how interventions with curriculum leaders can respond to relational patterns in their networks in ways that improve the relational space, creating better conditions for curriculum change to be realised.

The unfurling frond of a silver fern that graces the cover of this book is known in Aotearoa New Zealand as a 'koru'. The koru symbolises new life, growth and strength; ideas that are at the heart of the work we share about curriculum change and leadership.

Our work sought to give curriculum leaders in two kāhui ako – or communities of learning – opportunities to breathe new life into the relational space in which they work; in particular, the various relationships between and amongst people. Our aim was to help them to recognise the importance of the relational space and to improve the social conditions for collaborative work. It also sought to grow relational ties within and across schools in ways that support them to function as professional learning networks (Brown & Poortman, 2017; Poortman, Brown, & Schildkamp, 2022) and to support teachers to enact curricula that make a difference in learners' lives. And finally, our work sought to give curriculum leaders the strength to do their work, by providing them insights into their network, and action planning tools to make improvements.

Curriculum change is a constant in educational contexts seeking to improve equity and excellence, but ambitious goals of curriculum reform are seldom fully realised. We argue that all too often very little attention is paid to the relational space in which those reform ideas land. Strong (together with weak) relational ties amongst all of those involved within and across schools are critical for the success of curriculum reform. And curriculum leaders, as we see it, share responsibility not just for the content and enactment of curriculum, but also for the relational space in which that work takes place. This work recognises that the social processes involved in change stretch across individuals and levels within a system. It shifts the perspective from a focus on the individual and their attributes to the dynamics of a larger social network; the constellation of relationships amongst educators that give life to curriculum change and that support teachers to improve learners' experience of curriculum. The intervention we share in this book, therefore, aimed to support the leaders involved to make positive change in the relational aspects of their schools and wider network, to improve the conditions that are essential for aspirations of curriculum reforms to be realised.

Many change agents traditionally focus their improvement efforts on formal structures, processes and accountability levers. We supported these curriculum leaders to improve the relational linkages between individuals through which curriculum change can move.

While social network interventions are increasingly recognised as critical to educational improvement, often there is silence on the detail of intervention approaches and the underpinning theories that give rise to them. In this book, our aim is to make our intervention approach transparent so that others can draw on and adapt it in ways that are relevant in their own contexts.

In Part 1, we introduce the concept of social capital and highlight its relevance to curriculum improvement and curriculum realisation efforts. We contextualise our work in relation to social network interventions in contexts beyond education. We then introduce the particular theory of action approach we use to explain our intervention approach and describe how we collected and analysed data to give insight into shifts in the relational space in the two networks we worked with.

In Part 2, we make visible what we did, how and why. First, we present the big picture of our approach, and next we detail the purpose and activities of four *hui*, or gatherings, of curriculum leaders. The first hui was to provide *grounded stimulus* by engaging our participants with theoretical, conceptual and empirical insights relating to social capital, social networks and collaboration. The second hui saw our participants working together through a *guided discovery* process, engaging with maps and statistics from a social network survey of their own network, which provided a focus for a problem-solving approach. Our curriculum leaders agreed on problematic patterns to be the focus of action plans for improvement, offered ideas about the causes of those patterns, and proposed solutions logically linked to those causes. In the third hui, we worked with leaders from one network to refine their plan and to provide feedback on their leadership approach. In the final hui, we used a step-back consultancy process whereby each network took on the action plan of the other, in a way that gave rise to diverse perspectives about how to improve it.

Part 3 sets out the results of our efforts – and especially those of curriculum leaders who engaged deeply with this work. In the year and a half between time 1 and time 2 administrations of the social network survey, and following the four hui that comprised our intervention, the data showed a range of promising shifts. In this section, we detail how the relational infrastructure supporting curriculum change has been strengthened in the kāhui ako we worked with. These relational shifts are headed in the right direction and suggest the strengthening of social capital that will serve curriculum realisation efforts well. In closing, we reflect on key things we learned from an intervention perspective and present those as a network of social network intervention considerations.

PART 1

SETTING THE SCENE

Intervening on social networks is important because they exert powerful influences on the way people feel and behave. These effects can be observed in families, friendship networks and workplaces as well as in many other contexts. For example, people are more likely to become happy if their friends are happy and more likely to quit smoking if their friends do (Christakis & Fowler, 2013; Fowler & Christakis, 2008). In the workplace, employee wellbeing increases when colleagues receive leadership coaching (O'Connor & Cavanagh, 2013), and people are more likely to seek advice from a colleague who is similar to them (Cross, Borgatti, & Parker, 2001). In schools, social networks influence innovation (Liou & Daly, 2018a), the improvement of teaching practice (Sinnema, Liou, Daly, Cann, & Rodway, 2021) and curriculum and policy implementation (Coburn & Russell, 2008; Hopkins, Ozimek, & Sweet, 2017).

The potential for these kinds of impacts was the impetus for the Better Together intervention at the heart of this book, and in this part, we set the scene for our project. First, we provide theoretical context. Chapter 1 presents a social network lens on the work of curriculum realisation, highlighting how the relational space impacts on the success of curriculum reform. We use the term realisation to refer to the aspirations of curriculum change impacting changes in practice in schools and classrooms, and learners experiencing the curriculum in line with those aspirations. We introduce, in Chapter 2, the empirical context; we outline approaches that have been taken to social network interventions in the field of health, business and education. We also propose a framework for the use of data in social network interventions in education. In Chapter 3, we focus on the theoretical and conceptual context explaining the theory of action approach used throughout the book to describe our intervention. Finally, we turn to the practical context introducing the policy and practice landscape of our project in Chapter 4.

1

A SOCIAL NETWORK LENS ON CURRICULUM REALISATION

Central to educational improvement efforts is the improvement of curriculum policies that set out aspirations for learners and the realisation of those policies in practice. We refer here to the formal curriculum; the policies or plans – be they at national, provincial/regional or school level – documenting what learners should learn and what teachers' practice should address. The approach to and detail of curriculum policies varies across nations and jurisdictions, but they do share many common elements. These include, depending on the orientation of the curriculum: statements of vision or purpose; important principles or values; subjects or areas of learning; objectives, goals, learning outcomes or standards of some sort; and, increasingly, other cross-cutting elements such as skills, competencies, capabilities or cross-cutting themes. They also typically outline progression in some way, for example in relation to stages, phases, levels, or steps to which the former elements apply.

In the broad field of educational improvement, a central question of concern is: What should be improved? While many improvement efforts focus on teachers and teaching, on leaders and leading, or on schools and schooling, they all share an ultimate concern for improvements for learners and learning. In this sense, the curriculum becomes critical because curricula convey aspirations for learners in the present and for their future; they set out learners' curriculum entitlement. A curriculum is, therefore, an essential tool for determining priorities in educational improvement efforts and for assessing the effectiveness of those efforts.

Curricula are not only essential – but also contested and, as Wood (2021) describes, fiercely so. They are complex to design and are 'a product of contending social, political and historical forces' (p. 55). Curriculum reforms, like other educational reforms,

> have particular histories, and all of them are driven
> not only by technical considerations but also
> profoundly by cultural, political, and economic
> projects and by ideological and valuative visions
> of what schools should do and whom they should
> serve. (Apple, 2015, p. 1079)

This landscape of curriculum aspiration, entitlement and contestation has far-reaching implications for the networks of educators charged with realising a curriculum in their day-to-day work. It also results in curriculum change being a constant in the work of educational practitioners (including teachers, teaching assistants and leaders), policy-makers and researchers. We use the term *curriculum change* since it encompasses both curriculum reform instigated at system levels, and changes to elements of a curriculum, or instigated by those in schools and other educational settings. Curriculum change is constant because, in any given jurisdiction at any time, educationalists are likely to be either in the middle of curriculum change, looking towards it, or having recently gone through it, and grappling with the practice implications of the change. They are constantly amidst the ebb and flow of curriculum (Sinnema, 2016).

FORMS OF CURRICULUM CHANGE

Curriculum change takes various forms, including changes to curriculum orientations, roles and elements. Here, we turn to each of those forms of change, policy changes that need to be realised in practice; and unpack what they mean and where we see examples of them.

Changes to Curriculum Orientation

Curriculum change often involves adjustments to the orientation of a curriculum. The recent Australian curriculum, for example, has an orientation towards achievement standards (that describe what children should typically demonstrate) as well as level descriptions and content elaborations. In England, we see a focus on attainment targets, as set out in programmes of study levelled for all subjects at four key stages. In contrast, the *New Zealand Curriculum* (Ministry of Education, 2007) refresh is changing from levelled achievement objectives to a progression-focussed curriculum that sets out learning across five phases of learning throughout schooling. In Wales, the orientation is slightly different; 'what matters' statements are applied for each area of learning and experience and four purposes orient the curriculum towards much longer-term aspirations than was previously the case.

Changes to Curriculum Roles

In many jurisdictions, curriculum change involves shifts in the autonomy of those in various roles for curriculum decisions and design. As national curricula become either more or less flexible, practitioners' autonomy is altered. Educators find themselves, in many cases, with newfound authority to be involved in, and/or responsible for, not only the 'delivery' of curriculum but also its design – its shape, structure and content. This has been the case in contexts such as New Zealand (Sinnema, 2016; Sinnema & Aitken, 2013), Wales (Newton, 2020), Finland (Pietarinen, Pyhältö, & Soini, 2017) and Estonia (Mikser, Kärner, & Krull, 2016). In Wales, also, new roles have resulted from the government's adoption of a principle of subsidiarity for their recent curriculum reform to 'encourage teacher professionalism; stimulate improvements in teaching; enhance the responsiveness of schools to local and national needs; lead to increased confidence in the reforms' (Newton, 2020, p. 215). The subsidiarity principle sees curriculum created from the bottom up (Hughes & Lewis, 2020); practitioners are given responsibility for the process and there is 'local ownership and responsibility within a clear national framework of expectation and support' (Donaldson, 2015, p. 99). Those in roles close to the teaching and learning process have much greater authority for decision making and curriculum design than has ever been the case before.

Curriculum change can also have implications for the roles that stakeholders have in curriculum design for schools. The *New Zealand Curriculum* (New Zealand Ministry of Education, 2007) promoted parent and community roles in curriculum making in much more meaningful ways than was the case prior. Schools were encouraged, as part of the emphasis on the local curriculum, to partner with parents and local communities as co-constructors of and contributors to curriculum, alongside educational practitioners (Sinnema & Aitken, 2013).

The direction of change in other contexts (e.g. Australia, England) has been the opposite with tightly defined programmes of study. In some contexts, curriculum autonomy is limited as systems impose 'oppressive regimes of testing and inspection' resulting in reduced opportunity for teachers to shape curricula (Erss, 2018, p. 238). Such changes, like the tide, can ebb and flow as curriculum policies gravitate towards and away from autonomy across cycles of curriculum reform (Sinnema, 2016).

Changes to Curriculum Elements and Their Relationships

Curriculum change typically involves new or altered curriculum elements and/or new relationships of those elements with each other. For example, in Australia's recent curriculum reform, three dimensions are central to the national curriculum design (eight learning areas, cross-curriculum priorities and general capabilities). Those dimensions are unpacked with content descriptions (essential knowledge, understanding and skills). In New Zealand, curriculum refresh work is using an 'understand–know–do' framework with the intention to convey how students deepen their understanding of big ideas as they explore context (know) using inquiry practices (do) relevant to the learning area.

CURRICULUM CHANGE AND SOCIAL CAPITAL

Changes to curricula – whether to the orientation, roles or elements of curricula – all have implications for what teachers, individually, need to know, understand and do. But more importantly, they have implications for how networks of educators and others must work together, harnessing their collective potential, to respond to the curriculum change. In this work, we set out considerations pertinent to these forms of curriculum change with particular attention to social capital theory while also taking a social network perspective. Before we do that, we introduce two key concepts of social capital, bonding and bridging, as they relate to networks of educators going about curriculum-related work.

What Is Social Capital? The Seminal Examples

Social capital is widely understood as 'the intangible resources of community, shared values and trust that people draw on in daily life' and consists of 'personal connections and interpersonal interaction, together with the shared sets of values that are associated with these contacts' (Field, 2017, p. 3). It refers to the resources embedded in those social relations and structures that can be mobilised when someone wants to increase the likelihood of success in a purposive action (Lin, 2001). In the context of curriculum change, those *resources* might encompass knowledge and expertise in curriculum design, pedagogy or assessment. *Purposive actions* could involve curriculum design, problem solving or enactment at the system, school or classroom level.

While there are a number of important theorists in this field of social capital (Bourdieu, 1986; Bourdieu & Passeron, 1977; Field, 2017; Putnam, 1993, 2000) we turn to Coleman's (1988) seminal work to highlight important elements of social capital, because it connects specifically to education. He highlights how social structures allow high trust exchange, how shared norms provide a source of social capital and how social relations can create obligations. Below, we draw on Coleman's examples to propose illustrations of those elements of social capital with a curriculum context in mind.

THE MERCHANT'S BAG OF STONES EXAMPLE – SOCIAL STRUCTURES THAT ALLOW HIGH TRUST EXCHANGE

Coleman shares the example of a merchant who, during the course of negotiating a sale,

> *will hand over to another merchant a bag of stones for the latter to examine in private at his leisure, with no formal insurance that the latter will not substitute one or more inferior stones or a paste replica. (Coleman, 1988, p. 98)*

The willingness to hand over such valuable assets without any bond or insurance, and the taken-for-granted resulting trustworthiness, Coleman explains, form the attributes of the social structure. Such attributes arise from close family community or shared religious affiliations. We imagine the idea of high-trust exchange in the context of curriculum change in the following illustration:

Teacher A is in the process of preparing an application for a within-school curriculum leadership role, newly established to support the introduction of a new curriculum. Teacher B shares her own CV and curriculum portfolio from her own similar application in another context with Teacher A. No formal expectation is set out about how the material should be used, but there is enough trust in the relationship that Teacher B knows Teacher A will use the material appropriately and wants to help her out.

THE MOVING HOME EXAMPLE – NORMS THAT PROVIDE A SOURCE OF SOCIAL CAPITAL

In his example of a mother of six moving her family from suburban Detroit to Jerusalem so that her children can have greater freedoms, Coleman (1988) conveys the role of the normative structure and the social capital it makes available to families. The mother

> *felt safe in letting her eight year old take the six year old across town to school on the city bus and felt her children to be safe in playing without supervision in a city park, neither of which she felt able to do where she lived before. (p. 99)*

We can conceive of similar kinds of norms amongst those involved in curriculum change, for example:

Teacher C recently moved to Riverside School taking on the curriculum leadership role of Team Kea, a team of six teachers. In her previous school, everyone was expected to follow the same plan and use the same resources, activities and assessment tasks. Furthermore, their adherence to the plan was closely monitored. At her new school, there are quite different norms – while unit objectives are agreed upon and shared by the whole team, each teacher has the freedom to approach the teaching towards them quite differently. Inevitably teachers need help as they explore different approaches with varying success. Team Kea and others beyond are available to share, support and learn with them.

THE KAHN EL KHALILI MARKET EXAMPLE –
THE CREATION OF OBLIGATION IN
SOCIAL RELATIONS

Perhaps the most well-known of Coleman's (1988) examples of social capital is the one focussed on the Kahn El Khalili market of Cairo, in which he explains the social relations between merchants, which are difficult for outsiders to discern and which create a sense of obligation:

> *The owner of a shop that specialises in leather will, when queried about where one can find a certain kind of jewellery, turn out to sell that as well–or, what appears to be nearly the same thing, to have a close associate who sells it, to whom he will immediately take the customer. Or he will instantly become a money changer, although he is not a money changer, merely by turning to his colleague a few shops down. For some activities, such as bringing a customer to a friend's store, there are commissions; for others, such as money changing, merely the creation of obligation. (p. 99)*

What might such obligation in social relations look like in a curriculum-change context? We imagine that in the following illustration:

The Kowhai community of learning is a newly formed cluster of seven primary schools and one secondary school. Andrew, the principal of School A, shared a challenge he was facing with Barbara, the principal of School B: an integrated approach to curriculum had been put in place for some time, but evidence suggested their approach to leading this initiative was not yet successful. Learners were not developing important disciplinary knowledge, a particular problem in science.

Barbara knew that Colin, the principal of School C, had made impressive innovations and had success in their science programme and would have useful insights for Andrew. She had generously helped Colin on a similarly challenging, but unrelated, matter, and so felt sure Colin would be willing (and likely feel obliged if she asked) to share his experience with Andrew. She introduced them with this in mind.

These notions of social capital highlight the need to think of schools and networks of schools going about curriculum change, as complex organisations operating as professional learning networks, and in which all individuals have many diverse others to draw on in ways that benefit them all. The relational ties amongst them can be construed as either bonding or bridging.

Bonding and Bridging

Bonding social capital involves connections *within* a group or community – those who belong to the group are highly similar either in demographics, background, attitudes, interests, available resources and other characteristics (Claridge, 2018, p. 2). Bonding social capital 'exists between "people like us" who are "in it together" and who typically have strong close relationships' (Claridge, 2018, p. 2). Families, close friendship groups and groups of neighbours are examples of groups in which there are often highly dense relationships and strong bonding. From the point of view of curriculum change, we might see such bonding social capital amongst those who belong to the same school, same department or to a common curriculum working group, or with responsibility for a common cohort of students. It exists amongst those who know each other well and creates norms and trust that enable them to turn to each other on curriculum-related matters.

Bridging social capital, on the other hand, occurs in connections that link people from communities, groups or organisations that might otherwise be divided. It occurs across boundaries that can divide, including race, class and religion (Claridge, 2018). It is important, Claridge (2018) explains, because bridging social capital can allow access to information and power, leading to new opportunities, and can increase tolerance across diverse people and the exchange of information and ideas. With curriculum change in mind, bridging social capital is important, for example, to ensure those across disciplinary boundaries are connected (e.g. science or mathematics teachers connected to art or English teachers), to ensure those with different types of responsibility are connected (e.g. school counsellors connected to the form teachers or classroom teachers connected to those holding leadership roles) and to ensure connections across educational sectors (e.g. connections between those in early childhood, primary and secondary contexts).

Bridging social capital is known to increase tolerance and acceptance of different people, values and beliefs through contact with diverse others (Paxton, 2002), and to be supportive of innovation through the exchange of resources between groups with diverse interests (Daly & Finnigan, 2011). Furthermore, it can act as 'social leverage' (Putnam, 2000) and involves weak ties that are of strategic importance for bridging different groups (Granovetter, 1973). Such diversity, innovation and leverage are all essential to the work of curriculum change. Through bridging ties, resources associated with curriculum-change efforts held by each party can be shared and used to benefit all. Think, for example, of ideas and experiences being exchanged, as well as the tangible materials and resources that bring a curriculum to life.

Trust

While both bonding and bridging forms of social capital are associated with trust, insights from Patulny and Svendsen (2007) highlight how the nature of that trust differs. Bonding social capital is associated with particularised trust. While beneficial – exchange of resources within groups is important for curriculum-change efforts – this kind of trust can also result in more concern for the exchange of resources that benefit the group's own, rather than wider, interests. Bridging social capital, conversely, is associated more typically with generalised trust, the kind of trust that allows diverse people to meet, interact and share in a way that works with, not against, the system – critical in the context of curriculum change given the notion of curriculum entitlement that seeks to serve the wider good. Trust supports the development and maintenance of relations, often acting as the glue between bonding and bridging relationships (Bryk & Schneider, 2002).

FORMS OF CURRICULUM CHANGE AND THE ROLE OF BONDING AND BRIDGING

Next, we return to the forms of curriculum change introduced earlier (change to curriculum orientation, roles and elements), highlight examples of each form, and suggest implications of these changes in terms of both bonding and bridging ties.

Changed Curriculum Orientations

Bonding social capital is useful when changes in curriculum orientation occur because such changes position all educators, no matter their experience, as learners. The learning demands can create vulnerabilities that are well supported by the trust that allows even experienced educators to seek resources from others to support them to reorient their curriculum thinking and practice. Frequent interactions within a group associated with bonding social capital support teachers to operate simultaneously at multiple points along a novice–expert continuum – this 'novice and expert' (rather than 'novice or expert') profile is likely when curriculum orientations alter. In New Zealand's move to a progression-focussed curriculum, for example, those experienced in teaching at particular phases of learning (the senior, middle or junior school, for example) need to learn and understand progression across all phases of learning to support their response to curriculum.

Bridging social capital is also useful when a change in curriculum orientations occurs. When the orientation shifts to including or focussing on local curricula – as is the case in many recent curriculum reforms – issues and problem-centred approaches are often taken. These approaches require local community resources, so the more outward looking, inclusive and interconnected features of bridging social capital become important to ensure teachers can reach people in the community to bring those local insights to the curriculum learners' experience.

The need for bridging social capital is also well illustrated in curriculum reforms such as the International Baccalaureate. As Cohen and Mehta (2017) describe, the niche mission of this intellectually demanding and internationally oriented curriculum was supported by and demands bridging to resources outside the K-12 sector.

Changed Curriculum Roles

Bonding social capital is useful when practitioners' curriculum roles change in ways that not only give them permission, but also the responsibility, for designing local curricula. While the affordance of such responsibility is largely welcomed, for some, or at least sometimes, it can also be experienced as a burden (Sinnema, Nieveen, & Priestley, 2020). For some, the sense of burden arises from a lack of desire to take the responsibility afforded them or uncertainty about how to go about such a complex task. For others, while the responsibility and opportunity are welcome, the associated workload is not. An increasingly flexible curriculum policy can increase workload because 'it diminishes the value of, and market for, published resources; it presupposes expertise in curriculum that may not be widely or evenly spread' (Sinnema & Aitken, 2013, pp. 157–158).

Just as bonding social capital is useful for those suffering socioeconomic or health hardships, because it provides an important source of support (Claridge, 2018), so too it is helpful for teachers for whom newfound curriculum freedoms are an unwelcome weight on their shoulders. Bonding social capital – that which exists 'between "people like us" who are "in it together" and who typically have strong close relationships' (Claridge, 2018, p. 2) – provides a buffer: points of connection where teachers feel secure in sharing concerns and helping each other to respond.

Bonding social capital is also foregrounded in the move to system-level policies promoting flexibility in the design of local curricula. Such curricula are not just local because they *apply* to a particular school community, but are local because they are *developed collaboratively by* a range of stakeholders in that school community. In other words, it is not sufficient for each school just to *have* a local curriculum (one bought off a shelf, or developed by one/few of its members) but rather for it to have a local curriculum that has engaged people in various roles. Those roles extend beyond giving input or feedback to co-designing curriculum – a process that demands strong informal social relations characteristic of bonding social capital.

Bridging capital is useful when such change in curriculum roles occurs because new roles don't necessarily match existing expertise; inevitably new roles will not only reveal exciting new possibilities and practitioners' hidden talents, but will also surface limitations in their expertise – limitations in curriculum design might well be amongst them. Curriculum design is challenging, and even experts at the system level often struggle to design curricula that are understood, let alone implemented, as they intended (Hill, 2001). It is unlikely, therefore, that even highly experienced teachers have all of the expertise they could use given such skills are rarely addressed in teacher education or leadership-development initiatives. Good curriculum design demands expertise over and above expertise as a curriculum user or broader educational or pedagogical expertise. The role of a curriculum designer brings with it a need, as Aitken (2005) argues, for expertise in designing curricula that reduce extraneous cognitive load, and increase internal and external coherence (Shwartz, Weizman, Fortus, Krajcik, & Reiser, 2008). These are quite particular and sophisticated design skills, ones likely to be accessed through the support of those beyond existing networks. Furthermore, the entirety of the knowledge, skill set and perspectives required for developing a high-quality local curriculum is unlikely to exist in any one setting, even settings with broad and deep expertise. This highlights the importance of bridging capital.

When curriculum change demands that design processes involve communities, the need for boundary crossing becomes particularly marked. As Leat and Thomas (2018) explain,

> *schools are organisations with their own norms, practices and cultures. To engage with organisations or individuals from the community in the pursuit of locally generated curriculum provision, both schools and community partners face crossing boundaries. (p. 203)*

Changed Curriculum Elements

Bonding capital is useful when changes in curriculum elements challenge existing norms and demand collaborative action. New curriculum elements can have the knock-on effect of adding to curriculum overcrowding, intensifying the need for those with close bonds to work efficiently together in order to manage curriculum work and protect from overload. Bonding capital supports strong relationships amongst those in teaching teams, which can support them to navigate such changes; their bonds allow them to work efficiently together to address the change, and their shared specialist expertise or connections function as a resource for responding to the change.

Changes to curriculum elements can also create vulnerabilities as those who have considered themselves expert in their role suddenly feel novice in relation to new curriculum elements – this can create vulnerabilities and stress that are well supported through bonding capital, the strong ties with like-minded colleagues. An example from the New Zealand context is the embedding of a focus on strengthening literacy and numeracy in all subjects, not just English and mathematics, in the national qualification. Teachers who know themselves as experts in science, for example, have become responsible for the teaching of literacy and numeracy in ways that may, for some, lead to a sense of vulnerability, hence the potential for bonding social capital to be a source of support.

Bridging capital is useful when curriculum elements change in ways that demand practitioners develop new knowledge and skills. Curriculum-reform moves that push for curriculum integration, a feature of many new curricula, illustrate better than most changes that benefit from bridging social capital. Curriculum integration focusses on removing the boundaries between traditional subject specialisms, to enable more holistic and 'joined-up' learning opportunities (Kneen, Breeze, Davies-Barnes, John, & Thayer, 2020, p. 258). Examples abound, including in the most recent core curriculum of Finland where curriculum integration is compulsory, multi-disciplinary learning modules are a new element, and the curricula of the higher levels of schooling integrate content from across subjects (Niemela, 2021). Similarly, in South Africa, subject teachers have been called to integrate environmental education into their subject areas (Damoah & Adu, 2019); and, in Singapore, different disciplines within the arts (dance, music, drama and visual arts) have become integrated (Bautista, Tan, Ponnusamy, & Yau, 2016).

This increasing demand for curriculum integration suggests a parallel set of considerations for the network of educators charged with realising such curricula – it is not just the curriculum, or the content that must be integrated; so too must the people who teach those be integrated in some way. This means altering or removing boundaries in the ties between educators traditionally organised in subject specialisms. It means educators need more expansive and holistic networks with relational ties that support joined-up thinking amongst educators from previously siloed areas.

Some may mistakenly view the challenge of curriculum change to be largely up to individual teachers. But we know, for example from the work of Putwain and von der Embse (2019), that individual educators' self-efficacy is not enough to mitigate the stress associated with curriculum change. Their study of more than 800 teachers in English schools found that the advantages of self-efficacy moderated perceived stress which diminished as pressure from imposed curriculum changes became stronger. Personal resources such as self-efficacy, it would seem, are not sufficient, signalling the importance of curriculum leaders building and leveraging social capital to support curriculum-change efforts.

The efforts of bridging and bonding form networks of ties between and among educators as they go about their work. These networks are vital to for curricular efforts.

THE CRITICAL ROLE OF SOCIAL NETWORKS IN ADDRESSING THE CONSTRAINTS OF CURRICULUM CHANGE

Curriculum change initiatives often take a human capital perspective. In doing so, they address, for example, what each individual needs to know and understand, and the planning, teaching and assessment capabilities they might each need to have developed. Increasingly, education systems are recognising that more compelling approaches to ensuring the success of curriculum change are those that take a social capital perspective; this does not supplant attention on human capital, but supplements it so that both are working in concert. They recognise that it is in the social relations of the systems charged with realising curriculum policies that the resources needed to do that work exist. As Daly (2010) puts it, social capital is 'an investment in a system's social relations through which the resources of other individuals can be accessed, borrowed, or leveraged' (p. 4). Taking a social network perspective and paying attention to the informal webs of relationships is important, he explains, because it is those webs of relationships that are key determinants of 'how well and quickly change efforts take hold, diffuse, and sustain' (p. 3).

The implementation of changes to curriculum policies in many contexts over many decades has often been partially successful at best and unsuccessful at worst. And so, the call to pay attention to relationships and networks critical to reform success is both promising and timely. This suggests a need for work in the curriculum leadership space that shines a light on how networks and underpinning relational conditions can either constrain or support curriculum leaders' efforts.

In this book, we share an approach to intervention that does just that, following in the footsteps of those who have, over many decades, conducted social network interventions outside of education, and more recently in schooling and educational contexts.

2

SOCIAL NETWORK
INTERVENTIONS

This chapter explores how social network interventions can support people to leverage the power of social networks in support of their aspirations. Social network interventions

> *are purposeful efforts to use social networks or social network data to generate social influence, accelerate behavior change, improve performance, and/or achieve desirable outcomes among individuals, communities, organizations, or populations. (Valente, 2012, p. 49)*

We examine different approaches towards social network interventions and illustrate these with examples from a range of contexts before focussing on social network interventions in education.

APPROACHES TO SOCIAL NETWORK INTERVENTIONS

Social network interventions can differ in the approach they take and in particular in the way they respond to and/or use social network data. In a landmark paper, Valente (2012) outlines four approaches that nicely contrast these different approaches:

1. *identifying individuals* (to deliver or receive an intervention) on the basis of some network property

2. *segmentation*, where the intervention is directed towards groups of people

3. *induction*, where interactions between network members are encouraged or enhanced

4. *alteration*, where the intervention changes the network, for example by adding or deleting members or specific social ties.

Valente's classification has been used extensively in meta-analyses and systematic reviews of social network interventions in health (Hunter et al., 2019; Shelton et al., 2019) and in other fields; we use it to organise the examples of interventions we turn to next.

Approaches in the Health Field

Social network interventions have been used extensively in the field of health since the 1990s (Luke & Harris, 2007; Valente, 2010). They reflect all four of the approaches in Valente's (2012) classification outlined above and have been found to 'specifically use or alter the characteristics of social networks to generate, accelerate, or maintain health behaviours and positive health outcomes' (Hunter et al., 2019, p. 3).

Identifying Individuals

Many health-promoting interventions take the approach of identifying influential individuals within a health-related network (Valente, 2017). For example, social network data are used to identify key actors or opinion leaders – those most often nominated as a source of opinion by others in a network or deemed through analytic techniques to be most central. They are then trained to share health information, and in some cases matched in optimal combinations to mentees, in ways that speed up the diffusion of information across the network (Luke & Harris, 2007; Valente, 2010; Valente & Davis, 1999). In Sebire et al. (2018) work, for example, Year 8 girls identified by their peers as influential were trained to informally support their friends to increase their physical activity. The intervention showed promise in affecting girls' weekday moderate-to-vigorous physical activity.

The Segmentation Approach

Segmentation is also common in the health field where social network interventions respond to data from groups of people sharing a particular characteristic (rather than belonging to a particular organisation). They might be directed, for example, to women who have recently given birth, people who smoke, or those who use drugs (Shelton et al., 2019). Collecting whole network data for such groups can often be challenging and resource intensive, so many studies collect partial network data, such as ego-networks that represent social relations of one focal person (Shelton et al., 2019). Data can be derived from various sources, such as archived communications (e.g. phone or e-mail), publicly available information (e.g. social network platforms), participant observations and survey data (Shelton et al., 2019; Valente, 2010). This network data can then be used to inform health interventions.

The Induction Approach

Induction approaches to social network interventions focus on encouraging interactions between network members. They are common in health and are wide ranging in their targets, including improved behaviours relating to nutrition (Buller et al., 1999), physical activity (Gotsis, Wang, Spruijt-Metz, Jordan-Marsh, & Valente, 2013), health screening (Earp et al., 2002) and reduced risk-taking in sexual and drug-related behaviours such as, for example, smoking (Bastian et al., 2013). In Buller et al. (1999) work, for example, a peer-education type programme, which used the power of social networks to alter social group norms, led to dietary changes (increased fruit and vegetable intake) that persisted well beyond the conclusion of the intervention.

The Alteration Approach

Interventions that take an alteration approach encourage individuals to alter their social network, often expanding it through additional members who will support them and encourage desired behaviours. An example of this approach is seen in a project that assisted alcohol-dependent people to expand their social support network to include people who did not drink, which resulted in a much greater reduction in drinking than individuals who attended therapy sessions focussed on reducing drinking (Litt, Kadden, Kabela-Cormier, & Petry, 2007). Other alteration types of social network intervention include forming online communities to encourage smoking cessation (Lakon et al., 2016; Zhao et al., 2016) and introducing community health workers into the social networks of pregnant women to support them through pregnancy, delivery and the postpartum period (Adams, Nababan, & Hanifi, 2015).

These approaches to intervention can of course operate in combination, as in the example that Shelton et al. (2019) describe – opinion leaders within a network are carefully selected (identification approach) and trained to provide advice or support to others in the network (induction approach), about matters such as HIV prevention.

Approaches in the Workplace

Interventions with networks in workplace settings also serve various purposes – they might be for (1) promoting collaboration within a strategically important group; (2) building relationships across functional, geographical or hierarchical boundaries; and (3) integrating groups following a restructuring (Cross, Borgatti, & Parker, 2002). Often, they begin with organisational leaders inviting researchers to carry out social network analysis (SNA) to help with a problem they have observed. They can then work together, with leaders providing contextual information to help understand patterns discovered during the network analysis. Subsequent intervention can involve, and in some cases be driven by, those internal to the organisation, including, for example, formal leaders or human resource departments (Cross et al., 2002; Hatala & Lutta, 2009). Social network interventions in workplace settings also use the four intervention approaches illustrated above - identification of individuals, segmentation of groups, induction of new norms and alteration of networks.

The Identifying Individuals Approach

In some interventions, social network data are used to *identify individuals* with particular profiles, who might benefit from a particular intervention. The analysis might identify, for example, people with many connections in a network; they could then be interviewed to check if they are overburdened and establish if their workload should be reduced in some way (Cross et al., 2002). It might also identify those who would be suitable to place in 'knowledge champion' roles (Hatala & Lutta, 2009) given their influential position in a network. Conversely, if some employees are identified as having few connections in the network, then interventions might purposely include them in regular information sharing (Hatala & Lutta, 2009).

The Segmentation Approach

Some interventions target specific groups of people, identified through their role in an organisation, or, for larger organisations, through their membership of subdivisions. Once all members of the segment have been identified, a bounded-saturated approach (or full network census) can be used where every network member is invited to participate in the social network survey (Borgatti, Everett, & Johnson, 2018; Hanneman & Riddle, 2005; Lin, 1999; Scott, 2017).

The Induction Approach

Social network interventions aimed at establishing more frequent or stronger interactions between network members take an induction approach (Cross et al., 2002). For example, where a network analysis reveals subgroups within an organisation that rarely interact with each other, the organisation can implement initiatives to encourage the sharing of expertise between groups. They might implement, for example, a skill-profiling system to raise awareness of others' expertise or arrange opportunities for people to learn about projects that others are working on.

The Alteration Approach

Interventions that deliberately alter the network, through adding (or deleting) nodes and/or ties, are also common in commercial contexts. Similar to the induction approach that encourages greater interaction around specific topics, the alteration approach is often more deliberate in altering the network (Cross et al., 2002). The alteration might occur, for example, through intentionally staffing projects with members from different groups to ensure across-group collaboration, or constructing teams with relational profiles that vary in important ways.

Stimuli for Social Network Interventions: Maps
Statistics and Interview Insights

Social network interventions in workplaces, like in other contexts, often take advantage of social network data, and visualisations of networks called sociograms. These maps allow employees to respond to patterns of relationships in the network (see Figs. 1–3 for examples). Individuals (known as 'actors') are represented by a shape on the map, and the lines between them represent the relationships (or ties) between them.

Network maps can reveal strengths and problematic patterns of relationship. They might reveal, for example, a department that has two distinct subgroups that do not interact much, as we see in Fig. 1.

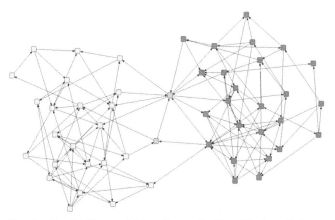

Fig. 1. Social Network Map Example: Two Distinct Subgroups Within One Department/Division.

Network maps might also reveal groups or departments that are isolated, poorly or well connected. In Fig. 2, we see that Group A is isolated from all other groups; there is only one tie between Groups C and D; and Groups B and D are the most well connected.

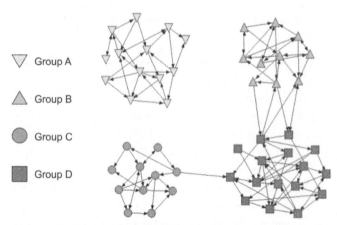

Fig. 2.   Social Network Map Example: Connectivity Between Groups/Departments/Divisions.

Alternatively, maps might show individuals who are in demand by others, but at risk of being a bottleneck, peripheral and at risk of disconnection, and/or brokers who connect otherwise disconnected others (see Fig. 3).

Network statistics accompanying such maps can provide intervention participants with a stimulus for their response.

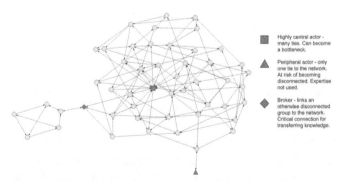

Fig. 3.   Social Network Map Example: Patterns Related to Individuals in the Network.

Table 1. Example SNA Statistics: Tie Density Within-Department and Between-Departments.

Department	A	B	C	D	E	F
Department A	55%					
Department B	2%	20%				
Department C	18%	12%	40%			
Department D	4%	4%	11%	33%		
Department E	7%	2%	14%	2%	77%	
Department F	2%	3%	21%	6%	4%	32%

Notes:

[Grey cells]   Within-department tie density

[White cells]   Between-department tie density

Such statistics might show patterns in tie density (the proportion of existing ties over possible ties expressed as a percentage). As we see in Table 1, network statistics can reveal where the highest density of ties with other departments lies (Department C), where there is the highest density of within-department ties (Department E), and where within-department density is lowest (Department B).

Social network data are often supplemented with other types of information that also provide insights into relational patterns and their causes. Insights might come through interviews with employees, through discussing network data with employees to understand possible cause, or through observing networks in action. Insights of this sort can be helpful in revealing drivers for the problematic patterns such as politics between groups, hierarchical leadership or processes that overload specific people and affect information flow. Insights of this sort are important since they can steer the direction for intervention and increase the chance of success.

Shaping Social Network Interventions

Intervention Activities

So, what kinds of intervention activities are often used? With a range of possible approaches available, and a range of stimuli to draw upon, what kinds of activities might social network interventionists turn to? The possibilities are limitless, but Table 2 sets out some possible examples according to the four approaches introduced earlier. In practice, of course, more than one approach will be reflected and interventions will be designed to suit the needs and strengths of those involved. Furthermore, the use of social network data in these activities should take seriously the need for ethical approaches to social network data collection and analysis (Tubaro, Ryan, Casilli, & D'Angelo, 2021).

To increase their chance of being impactful, social network interventions should not only respond to insights from social network data in proposing initiatives for participants, but also have their participants engage with the data about their very own networks. In this way, a network intervention is a very reciprocal process that involves interventionists and participants in a deep dialogue. This proposition is supported in the contrasting findings of two studies – one by Cross et al. (2002) and another by Hatala and Lutta (2009). In the Cross et al. (2002) study, a facilitated group discussion took place focussed on network maps showing two distinct subgroups in one department. The discussion led to a range of interventions and, 9 months later, network maps showing a well-integrated rather than divided group (Cross et al., 2002). In contrast, Hatala and Lutta (2009) work describes an approach whereby social network data were used by researchers (not participants) who then suggested a range of interventions aimed at information sharing in the organisation. Participants selected some of those interventions to implement, but there was minimal impact on information sharing.

Table 2. Intervention Activity Examples for Valente's Four Intervention Approaches.

Identifying individuals	Segmentation
• Identifying employees who are very highly connected to others in order to check if they are overloaded with work and some tasks could be passed on to others • Identifying individuals who are not well connected to others and supporting them to become more integrated into the team • Identifying people who are highly central in a knowledge network and placing them in 'knowledge champion' roles • Sharing individual-level network maps (known as ego-networks) with employees and guiding them through reflective questions so they can assess the effectiveness of their personal network	• Identifying a particular group, such as executive leaders, and analysing their position in the network • Identifying groups where altered relational patterns would support their effectiveness • Comparing the relational activity of different groups on different types of relational tie (e.g. advice, energy, collaboration) to prioritise intervention activity

Induction	Alteration
Setting up systems to communicate what different groups and employees are working on in order to raise awareness of others' expertise Setting project goals and performance measurements that are linked to working across teams or collaborating with others Address political problems between groups through measures such as executive coaching and revised performance management practices	Creating communities of practice Staffing projects with members of different groups or departments to encourage building relationships between groups Constructing teams on the basis of people's network profiles, for example including on each team at least one member who is highly sought out for advice, and one who is considered by others to be highly energising Reconfiguring group membership to take advantage of identified strengths

THE USE OF SOCIAL NETWORK THEORY TO INFORM INTERVENTIONS IN EDUCATION

While the turn to social network perspectives is much more recent in education than in other sectors, education researchers and educators have increasingly been following in the footsteps of those working in this way in health and organisational studies, both with adults and young people. Social network interventions with young people have the potential to make a powerful impact on their lives. The work of DeLay et al. (2016), for example, used longitudinal SNA to examine the impact of a social-emotional learning intervention on elementary students. Through that analysis, they established that social-emotional learning interventions may change social processes in a classroom peer network, break down barriers of social segregation and improve academic performance.

In studies with educators in school settings, we see interventions that reflect two different orientations that are contrasted in Valente's 2012 definition of social network interventions. Some interventions purposefully use 'social networks' and others use 'social network data' to achieve their goals. In education, there is a tendency for interventions in the social network space to focus on using social networks themselves without the use of social network data.

In education, we often see social capital and social network theory used to inform interventions that aim to improve teachers' practice and thus outcomes for students. Examples include projects that focus on promoting collaboration to develop teachers' practice (Nijland, van Amersfoort, Schreurs, & de Laat, 2018; Van Waes, De Maeyer, Moolenaar, Van Petegem, & Van den Bossche, 2018; Woodland, Barry, & Roohr, 2014, Woodland, Douglas, & Matuszczak, 2021), or on professional development relating to particular curriculum areas or pedagogical approaches, where collaboration is a key feature of the programme (Baker-Doyle & Yoon, 2010; Yoon, 2022). Such interventions include system-wide programmes that bring together teachers from multiple schools (e.g. Yoon, Yom, Yang, & Liu, 2017), multischool collaboration projects initiated by schools (Nijland et al., 2018; Woodland et al., 2014, 2021) or university-based professional development programmes (Van Waes et al., 2018) and graduate courses (Liou & Daly, 2018b). While these kinds of interventions are strong in their engagement with social network and/or social capital theory, they vary in the extent to which they use social network *data*, our focus in the following section.

THE USE OF DATA IN SOCIAL NETWORK INTERVENTIONS IN EDUCATION

When social network data are used in interventions, approaches vary with regard to who gets to engage with them, who uses them and the purposes for which they are used. To illustrate these various approaches, we have developed a matrix of 'genres' of social network data use in interventions (see Fig. 4).

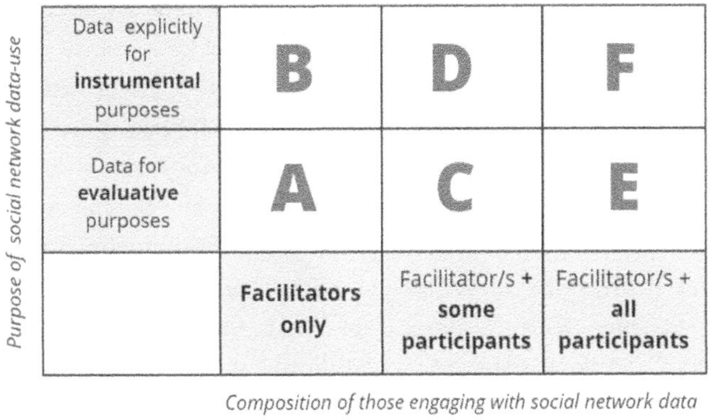

Purpose of social network data-use	Data explicitly for **instrumental** purposes	B	D	F
	Data for **evaluative** purposes	A	C	E
		Facilitators only	Facilitator/s + **some participants**	Facilitator/s + **all participants**

Composition of those engaging with social network data

Fig. 4. Genres of Approaches to SNA Data Use in Interventions.

At the intersection of two purposes of data use in social network interventions (evaluative and instrumental) and three compositions of data users (facilitator/s only; facilitator/s + some participants; and facilitator/s + all participants), we propose the six genres set out in Fig. 4 (Types A to F, detailed below). By evaluative purposes, we mean those that determine the success of an initiative or intervention. By instrumental purposes, we mean those that serve the practical needs of those whose social network was investigated, helping them, for example, design a response, make decisions or plan intentional action.

Type A Interventions

Type A interventions are those that are evaluated with network data that are used by facilitators/researchers only: The facilitator/s (or researchers) use social network analyses to evaluate changes in social relations resulting from a programme/intervention.

Often, interventions are focussed on things above and beyond the network itself (effective teaching in particular curriculum areas, for example) while network data are used to evaluate the impact of the intervention. An example of this genre is the work by Hopkins, Ozimek, and Sweet (2017) which explored the work of mathematics coaches in a system-wide effort to improve elementary mathematics education in a medium-sized suburban school district. While the intervention focussed on instructional coaching (leading both formal professional development and informal opportunities for teachers to learn about a new mathematics curriculum), social network data from 14 schools across 6 years were used to analyse the extent to which the mathematics coaches acted as brokers between school district offices and schools, and catalysts for collective inquiry.

We also see examples of Type A in a series of studies described by Yoon (2022). They used concepts from social capital to inform the design of an intervention aimed at improving relational ties amongst participants and used social network data to evaluate it. 'Seeding interactions' (connecting teachers proficient in the use of particular resources with teachers who were struggling) were used to improve tie quality of the social network. A 'birds of a feather' strategy saw teachers from similar schools grouped so that their conversations were meaningful to their particular context and therefore encouraged deep interactions. A strategy called 'expertise transparency' asked teachers to conduct professional development sessions on a topic in order to reveal hidden expertise in the network. These strategies were shown to almost double the number of interactions between project participants and to increase teacher confidence (Yoon, 2018).

Type B Interventions

Type B interventions involve facilitator/s (or researchers) engaging with network data for improvement purposes. The facilitators (or researchers) engage with social network analyses to inform the design of a programme/intervention; the activities respond in some way to social network data in an effort to improve the network.

Type B is illustrated in a study described by Baker-Doyle and Yoon (2010) in which facilitators actively and explicitly communicated teachers' expertise and encouraged network members to seek out experts. This was in response to learning, from analysis of network data, that teachers with the highest expertise scores were more isolated in the network than other members. They used a platform called 'Ning' which required teachers to post information about their background and expertise, allowed the teachers to communicate and facilitators to set assignments. The intervention resulted in increased communication among the teachers.

Type C Interventions

In Type C, facilitator/s and selected leaders evaluate the intervention using network data. Social network analyses are shared with a select group of participants, typically leaders, as part of the facilitator/s' (or researchers') evaluation of changes to social relations in a network.

Many studies that describe or evaluate relationality in networks do not involve explicit improvement-oriented interventions, but are likely to report findings to participants and/or leadership teams of schools and organisations involved. These interactions may not always be explicitly mentioned in publications about the work, but rather alluded to discussion of implications and/or researcher obligations set out in ethical consent processes. A study of the network formation, for example, used social network analyses to examine collaboration patterns in a network of schools transitioning from monolingual English to bilingual education (Scanlan, Kim, & Ludlow, 2019). The findings highlight a need for resources to be focussed on supporting educators to develop strong collegial networks both within and across schools, and find that mentors are the most powerful individuals who serve as critical friends to implementation teams. These findings are both relevant to the field and highly relevant to the practice of practitioners involved in this study.

The relevance of insights from social network analyses in helping schools to improve their knowledge brokerage in the context of sustainable school improvement efforts is also raised by van den Boom-Muilenburg et al. (2022). Their findings in relation to knowledge brokerage in professional learning communities (PLCs) found that experience, but less so for-mal position, was important for being a key actor in knowl-edge exchange. Key knowledge brokers also fit quite different profiles – highly relevant findings to those leading and engag-ing with the schools involved.

Type D Interventions

Type D interventions involve facilitator/s and some network members engaging with network data for improvement pur-poses. Facilitators (or researchers) share social network data with a select group of participants, typically leaders, and they respond either individually or collectively in ways that improve the network. These interventions provide insights that help people make decisions. For example, in the case of principals, their decision making about promotion, role-assignment or team construction responds to the social net-work data.

Type D is illustrated by Woodland et al. (2014) project, where social network data revealed two individuals in a school were particularly highly connected. When this pattern was discussed with the school principal, he shared that he had been considering promoting those people into coaching roles, and that the social network data confirmed for him the merits of that decision. In another project (Woodland et al., 2021), social network data revealed most grade-level teaching teams to be disconnected from teachers in the rest of the school. This analysis led the principal to create a new instructional leadership team with members from each grade level in order to increase collaboration across the school. These kinds of interventions show the utility of data on the relational ties in educational networks.

Type E Interventions

In Type E interventions, social network data are used by all in the network to evaluate it. For example, Nijland et al. (2018) collected social network data from teachers across five schools about which teachers they talked to in relation to particular topics. The maps generated from this data were displayed in each participating school for four weeks. Although the data were not used specifically to design particular interventions, they helped raise teachers' awareness of their networks and provided insights into other people interested in particular topics.

Sharing network data with all participants helps to generate network awareness amongst them. That was the case in Liou and Daly (2018b) work in a graduate-teacher education programme, which used a cohort-based course design with collaborative learning. Teacher candidates participated in a two-hour workshop on social networks that included sharing social network data collected from these teacher candidates at the beginning of the programme. The workshop was designed to raise their awareness of the importance of the social network ties necessary for their learning. While the social network data did not lead to (re)design of the teacher education programme (e.g. altering membership of cohorts) it was intended to influence the structure of the network. Over the course of the 10-month programme, while the total number of ties decreased, reciprocity increased, and ties became more focussed on subject cohorts, suggesting that the teacher candidates may have become more purposively selective about their ties.

Type F Interventions

Type F interventions involve facilitator/s and all network members engaging with network data for improvement purposes In this way, they all have the opportunity to respond either individually or collectively in ways that improve the network. While Type F is much less common than other types, it is a very important genre of social network intervention studies. When network data visualisations are shared with all intervention participants, everyone can make informed decisions about their own network and the network as a whole (Baker-Doyle & Yoon, 2020). It allows them to respond intentionally. There is much potential in education for the sharing of network data in this way, as has been the case in successful social network interventions in the organisational change field (Cross et al., 2002).

In most cases, these interventions involve a collective (but not collaborative) approach to the engagement with and response to data. An example of collective intentional network action can be seen in the Van Waes et al. (2018) study with 22 novice university teachers. They all completed a social network survey from which ego-network maps of their individual teaching network were constructed. The survey had asked them to indicate whom they discussed instructional practice with and whom they went to for information and advice. The intervention involved sessions in which teachers learned about network concepts and were supported to analyse their network's composition. They considered, for example, the diversity of the expertise in their network and the extent to which ties are held with those beyond their own department. This kind of engagement with social network data, and further training in the programme, led the teachers to intentionally 'rewire' their network so that its potential could be realised. Compared to a control group in a teaching professional development programme that did not involve engaging or responding to network data, the participants in this intervention increased the size and diversity of their networks.

Far less often, interventions in this genre use data for intentional network action in a collaborative way. Rich discussions, for example, can be stimulated by showing network maps to the members of a group and asking them to diagnose the patterns they see, as well as the issues facilitating or impeding their effectiveness. Often, this process simultaneously creates common awareness of problems, helps define solutions and gains agreement on actions – all critical steps to effecting organisational change.

The Better Together intervention – the focus of the rest of this book – did just this by inviting intentional collaborative network action in response to network data shared with all network members so that they could work together on understanding and improving their relational space. Our Type F approach is described and explained using a theory of action approach; and, in the next chapter, we make explicit what this approach entails.

3

A THEORY OF ACTION
APPROACH TO EXAMINING
INTERVENTIONS

We describe and explain our Better Together intervention in Chapter 6, and throughout the book, in a way that we hope will make it actionable for others; we use a theory of action approach to convey what we did. We also used a theory of action approach directly in our work with some of the curriculum leaders involved in the project. Because it is a prominent frame in our intervention practice, and because the term *theory of action* is used with different interpretations in different contexts, it needs some introduction. In this chapter, therefore, we explain in general terms what *we* mean by a theory of action approach, drawing mainly on the work of Argyris and Schön (1974) and Robinson (1993). With this introduction, we hope to orient readers to our way of framing the intervention and potentially to stimulate a frame for the design of others' interventions.

OUR THEORY OF ACTION APPROACH: ATTENTION TO ACTIONS, CONSTRAINTS AND CONSEQUENCES

The term 'theory of action' has been widely used, but in many different ways since Argyris and Schön first coined the phrase in 1974. We draw on Robinson's (1993) description of theories of action as solutions to problems. Problems comprise a demand something be done about something (e.g. a wish to test an intervention to improve a social network) and a set of conditions that 'establish the parameters of acceptable solutions' (p. 28).

We use the three theory-of-action components – actions, constraints and consequences – in the theory-of-action maps in which we describe our intervention practice. *Actions*, in a theory of action approach, represent solutions to problems of practice. The actions we outline are our solutions to the problem of how to intervene with educational leaders in ways that help them improve their network. The actions are not random – we chose them because they met conditions governing our practice – what Robinson refers to as *constraints*. We also outline the *consequences* of our actions in relation to our goals and other impacts on participants and their networks.

The Notion of Constraints as Helpful

The term 'constraints', as we use it in relation to theories of action, has a meaning distinct from the common usage of the term. Constraints do not refer to something negative or signal barriers. Rather, constraints are positive because they help narrow down a vast array of possible actions to actions we actually take. Without constraints, the vast array of actions would be stifling. Constraints in such a conception refer to such things as goals or aims, beliefs, values, assumptions about self and others and attitudes; perceptions of institutional, legal, regulatory and resource requirements; and norms or routines (Robinson & Lai, 2005). Larger theories such as historic, political and racial theories are present but are represented in the understandings of individuals in their sense and decision making as they act (Hannah, Sinnema, & Robinson, 2021).

Constraints function as a set and often exist in tension – frequently considerable tension. They are satisfied as a set through the creative design of actions, which seek to maintain those governing conditions within acceptable limits. Some constraints may be weighted as more important than others. In describing our theory of action approach, it is important to highlight that we see constraints as helpful in that they 'ruled in' certain actions, and where alternative actions violated constraints, those actions were ruled out.

WHY DESCRIBE OUR INTERVENTION USING A THEORY OF ACTION APPROACH?

Theory of action approaches have been used in a range of educational contexts to describe, explain and inform improvement in educators' practice since Argyris and Schön's seminal work in the field (Argyris, 1976, 1993, 2008; Argyris & Schön, 1996). They have been used to provide insight into individual educational leaders' practice. For example, we see this in work relating to secondary school leaders' on-the-job decision making (Robinson & Donald, 2014), elementary school middle leaders' practice in attempting to solve problems of persistent reading underachievement (Patuawa, Robinson, Sinnema, & Zhu, 2021), Japanese educational leaders' approach to communicating student incidents to parents (Hannah, Sinnema, &

Robinson, 2018) and school leaders' approaches to problem-solving conversations with subordinates (Robinson, Meyer, Le Fevre, & Sinnema, 2020).

Theories of action have also been used to describe the actions of collectives, such as the collaborative practices amongst teachers in multi-school networks (Sinnema, Daly, Liou, & Rodway, 2020). We also see the value of theory of action descriptions of students' actions; take, for example, Peeters, Robinson, and Rubie-Davies (2020) work on students' help-seeking and avoidance when facing difficult mathematics classwork and Robinson and Lai's (1999) earlier work on tertiary students' practice of copying assignments.

Theories of action have been used less often to shed light on the practice of those in teacher education, despite the value of this evident in Peeters and Robinson's (2015) self-study work on a teacher educator's approach to facilitating teachers' more child-centred practice for improving students' literacy. It is a related space of teacher education, and in particular an intervention with in-service educators, that is the focus of this book.

Illuminating Intervention

We know that a great deal of education system resources is allocated to professional learning for educational leaders, including those with leadership responsibility for the curriculum. But we also see that there is very little published in the educational improvement field that provides rich and detailed insight into the practice of those leading (or even delivering) professional learning. Often descriptions are at an abstract or general level ('an intervention' or 'an intervention on "x"' is said to have happened), but there is little by way of detail and/or explicit description of programme activities, as promoted in programme evaluation standards (see, e.g. Yarbrough,

Shula, Hopson, & Caruthers, 2011). Such absence of detail makes the evaluation of professional learning programmes or interventions challenging for both those formally evaluating them and those reading about them. Even those who are just curious about (rather than evaluating) how interventions are carried out are often left in the dark.

We use the term *intervention* to describe the professional learning we did with curriculum leaders to mark out the fact that we were simultaneously leading professional learning for them and investigating our own professional learning approach. We call it an intervention because we paid attention to pre- and post-intervention data to provide insight into the impact of our practice. Those insights, we hope, will also be relevant to those who work in a space they refer to as professional learning. Although we are targeting these important system leaders, we posit that this approach is widely generalisable.

Theory of Action Maps: Pictures of Practice

As Fig. 5 shows, we describe *our* practice as interventionists – the action components of the theories of action we present focus on *our actions* and are set out in relation to the constraints that drive them. Any consequential actions of the practitioners we worked with are set out as consequences (rather than actions). We present these descriptions using theory of action maps or, as we referred to them in this project, 'pictures of practice'.

We take this approach in order to deprivatise the practice of intervention with educators. Deprivatising our practice

Fig. 5. Theory of Action Elements.

means we steer away from a limited account of practice (one that is private or vague) and move towards an account of practice that allows evaluation and is learning oriented – an account that is accessible, explanatory and actionable and enables those involved and those it is shared with to learn. Next, we unpack those aspects a little more.

An Accessible Account

Enabling readers to understand how success was achieved (or not) demands that theories of change – the term used to denote the theory of action concept more generally (Coryn, Noakes, Westine, & Schröter, 2011; Mayne, 2015) – make both general and more detailed description accessible. They must both capture the complexity of the practice they describe and be simple enough to be usable (Davies, 2018; Funnell & Rogers, 2011). Diagrammatic forms (Davies, 2018; Mayne, 2015; Stein & Valters, 2012) are often used in an effort to meet these dual requirements (Davies, 2018). Davies (2018) notes that although simplicity is important for readability and usability, 'sufficient detail, to ensure some match with the complexity of the real world … is essential if the Theory of Change is to be evaluable' (p. 440). Many of the theories of change Davies uses to exemplify typical problems are very complex diagrams, with multiple boxes representing events linked by multiple arrows representing connections between them. The problem as Davies describes it is how to accurately represent those connections between events; while simplicity might be needed to convey overall direction, evaluability requires detailed descriptions of events and their causal connections to be made accessible so that the logic can be examined and they are able to be falsified.

A relatively recent turn to making general and detailed aspects of intervention accessible, in ways that convey both complexity and simplicity, is in contrast to early evaluation work that tended to focus on the outcomes of interventions in terms of their impact on subjects. Kirkpatrick and Kirkpatrick's (2006) classic four-level model, for example, evaluates the impact of training interventions by assessing the reaction of the subjects to the intervention, its impact on their learning and behaviour and finally the impact of any changes on the organisation. Guskey (2002) advocates for a similar five-level framework for evaluating teacher professional development, in which the final step is the impact of interventions on teaching staff and on student performance. However, while such approaches to evaluation may help determine the efficacy of interventions, they provide rather less information on how success and failure comes about (Reio, Rocco, Smith, & Chang, 2017). As such, their utility as a means for summative assessment of an intervention itself is somewhat reduced.

An Explanatory Account

More contemporary approaches to intervention evaluation focus on the theory underpinning and driving interventions. The logic linking intervention activities and outcomes is emphasised rather than results (Davies, 2018); this logic provides a deeper and explanatory account. It specifies mechanisms for change within an intervention, making it easier to improve the robustness of the theory by integrating existing research and exploring alternative causal explanations (Rogers, 2007). More robust and explanatory theories of change are important because they enhance the scalability of an intervention (Mayne, 2017).

Theories of action provide explanatory accounts of practice and are also represented diagrammatically. They are carefully constructed to describe practice at a high and general level and in a way that represents particular practices but doesn't present all of the detail. The simplified nature of the theory of action diagrams is designed to focus specifically on the causality between constraints, actions that satisfy those constraints, and the consequences – intended and unintended – that result from the action. Their tripartite structure represents causal propositions that link the three components: in situation X, under conditions $C_1 \ldots C_n$, do Y in order to achieve goal Z (Argyris & Schön, 1974; Friedman & Putnam, 2014). Causality is implicit in the description of both of the three components and the linkages between them.

Such simplicity is important for the evaluation of theories of action, which are implemented as people go about designing and creating the world the theory of action imagines (Argyris, 1996). By clearly stating the causality involved, theories of action make themselves both usable and evaluable. The veracity of the causal claims made within the theory of action can be evaluated both in reflection-in-action and post hoc in reflection-on-action (Schön, 2017). Actions can be assessed on the degree to which they satisfy governing conditions; the accuracy of assumptions contained within governing conditions can be assessed by linking them to outcomes observed; and the effectiveness of an intervention can be evaluated as a whole.

An Actionable Account

Our intervention is not a perfect and complete recipe for others to follow to the letter. Rather, we present our approach as evidence of our learning and of a set of parameters with which others can engage. Drawing on a recipe metaphor, it is a 'recipe' that can be used by others as a source of inspiration; they might draw on it, but inevitably include different ingredients, in different conditions, with different tools available to them, and share with others with different tastes and preferences. But our account ought to be actionable by others; and it is only actionable when others can access both the general and more particular insights into what we did *and* be exposed to the theory and logic that explains the extent to which our work was successful. Only then can they consider the implications and possibilities for their own practice.

Making transparent the theory behind our actions and surfacing the causality involved allows others to evaluate its success in ways that might be useful to their own practice. Therefore, we focus not just on the results of our intervention, but on the reasoning that guided our actions and the link between our reasoning, our actions, and the consequences for others. This focus necessitates a way of describing what we did that provides a means for examining our logic and improving our intervention. Such a description is key to making our approach to intervention actionable for others (Argyris, 1996).

Achieving such actionability requires that we satisfy certain conditions. We need firstly to not only describe what is likely to happen under the conditions we specify, but also how people might create those conditions in the first place. Secondly, we need to demonstrate how the causality we describe leads to the intended consequences and not others. Finally, the theory of intervention we share should be usable under different conditions for different organisations; the generalisations we make should hold despite any variance in actions taken by different interventionists in different contexts. Describing our intervention is key to its 'adaptive integration' so as to meet local conditions in the different contexts it might be used in.

In the next chapter, we offer a taste of the particular educational context in which the intervention this book focusses on took place, in Aotearoa New Zealand.

4

THE POLICY LANDSCAPE AND
THE PROJECT CONTEXT

We illustrate approaches to intervention for improving curriculum leadership through a recent project, the Better Together project, for curriculum leaders in Aotearoa New Zealand. We had the pleasure of designing an intervention to support curriculum leaders in a range of roles, from diverse contexts, to lead their teams in ways that would support the improvement of curriculum, teaching and learning. We opted not to do that by directly teaching them about curriculum, or teaching and learning, but rather by supporting them to improve the relational space in which *their* efforts to improve curriculum, teaching and learning take place. In other words, working on the social conditions that are necessary for other important work to occur. In doing so, we took a social, rather than a purely human capital approach.

THE POLICY CONTEXT

Before we describe the project, we introduce the educational policy context within which the project took place and how the project approach connected with that context.

Kāhui Ako

The schools and teachers involved in the Better Together project were from two communities of learning, or kāhui ako (New Zealand Ministry of Education, 2014) as they are known in Aotearoa New Zealand. Kāhui ako, like similar policies and initiatives in other countries, treat educational improvement as a collective concern and recognise pre-existing expertise that can be leveraged in ways that support improved teaching and learning. Kāhui ako bring groups of schools, typically close in proximity, together to define shared achievement challenges and to work on addressing them. Our interest in attending to social capital is consistent with key underpinnings of the kāhui ako policy – a policy that has privileged relational trust, intergroup leadership, teacher leadership and goal interdependence (Sinnema, Hannah, Finnerty, & Daly, 2021).

In terms of relational trust, the kāhui ako policy has seen schools that were previously disconnected, despite their physical proximity, become interconnected; interconnected by educational goals (including goals for priority learners), by leadership roles (with an intention for across-school leads to lead teachers in schools other than their own) and by resources (sharing funding for network activity). In this way, they can function as a professional learning network (Brown & Poortman, 2017; Schnellert, 2020). Interconnectedness of this sort demands high levels of relational trust, in other words, the kind of respect, competence, personal regard for others and integrity that Bryk and Schneider (2002) describe. Educators from across schools in a kāhui ako need a sense that their ideas and contributions are heard and valued (*respect*); parties need to trust that others have sufficient *competence* to carry out their roles; there needs to be a level of care and concern for the needs of others that invites reciprocity (*personal regard for others*); and they need to trust others will do as they say (*integrity*). These qualities, while idealistic, can be challenging to enact amongst educators within schools and can be even challenging (but also very rewarding) when occurring amongst educators from different schools that have formerly been somewhat in competition.

The kāhui ako policy has an emphasis on intergroup leadership – a principal from one of the member schools is appointed to lead each network – hence widening the scope of leaders' traditional responsibility and influence. It also emphasises teacher leadership beyond traditional teacher leadership boundaries through the appointment of across-school lead teacher roles (typically between one and three teachers per kāhui ako). Those in these roles are responsible for supporting improvement in student achievement and well-being by strengthening teaching practice. They are expected to share their skills and knowledge and carry out cycles of inquiry and improvement across the kāhui ako. In addition, these lead teacher roles support career progression given that they are assigned to those not already holding school-based leadership positions (e.g. associate or deputy principals). Within-school lead teachers are also appointed; they are also charged with promoting best teaching practice and strengthening inquiry and are expected to work with other teachers from schools other than their own to respond to challenges in practice. While kāhui ako role descriptions do not explicitly refer to social capital, it is prominent in an implicit way in the policy's emphasis on educators working across schools as they collaborate on improvement initiatives.

Another important feature of the policy is its attempt at using the power of goal interdependence, through the requirement for kāhui ako to determine shared achievement challenges for all member schools to work on. While the intention here is good, in practice, there has not always been true interdependence (Beverborg, Sleegers, Moolenaar, & van Veen, 2020). Instead, typically, goals relevant to each in a kāhui ako are presented together, but do not really create interdependence (Sinnema, Hannah et al., 2021) – for example, particular goals for the secondary school/s in the network and other goals for the primary schools. Such goals, while conveyed as belonging to the entire network, do not require the kind of co-ordinated effort that might activate the potential for goal interdependence. In addition, the scope and nature of goals, particularly in the early stages of the policy, were largely determined centrally; there was a requirement that kāhui ako goals focussed on particular aspects of learning (literacy and numeracy) and particular learners (priority learners). Many kāhui ako aspired to focus on alternate goals, or related but differently framed goals, potentially reducing the commitment to collective effort towards the goals they were required to have.

An intention of our project was for social capital and the functioning of the network itself to be in the frame as a target for their goals; our aim was to make existing patterns visible in the network in a way that stimulated alternative patterns to be a shared goal amongst curriculum leaders across schools and the wider network. The leaders in our project held a range of formal and informal leadership roles, with expertise in curriculum broadly, and in particular areas of learning. In this sense, we hope our work speaks to diverse curriculum leaders in a range of contexts.

The Leadership Capability Framework

The conception of leadership in our project recognised that improvement should be deeply grounded in the social aspect of leadership work. That conception is consistent with leadership policy in Aotearoa New Zealand and, in particular, with the country's educational leadership capability framework (Education Council of Aotearoa New Zealand, 2018). Our focus on the role curriculum leaders should play in strengthening the relational space is consistent with at least five capabilities in the framework. The first involves 'building and sustaining collective leadership and professional community'. It recognises that effective learning happens when teachers work together to share their knowledge. The social network methodology we used allowed us and our leader participants a deep understanding of how teachers were working together and sharing knowledge. The social network analysis (SNA) approach we used, gathering insights from a high proportion of educators across each kāhui ako, allowed us to establish the extent to which teachers work together and share knowledge. Rather than relying on a collation of individuals' perceptions of relational ties across the network, we were able to reveal a robust picture of relational patterns based on all of their accounts of actual ties with others in the network. Our social network survey tool asked respondents, for example, how frequently they turn to all others in the network for advice about curriculum or to collaborate to design or refine curriculum. It asked about all of the people they typically 'go to' for expertise to help them address curriculum problems or turn to for curriculum-related resources or materials. We were then able to analyse a range of cohesion and centrality measures that we introduce in the next chapter.

Secondly, the framework refers to leaders as 'he kaikōtuitui' (the networker); that is, as people who 'network, broker and facilitate relationships that contribute towards achieving organisational goals'. Our analyses, detailed in a later chapter, paid attention to networking, brokerage (connecting disconnected others) and facilitation of relationships at the network level in a way that provides insight into the relational space referred to here.

Thirdly, the framework refers to leaders as 'he kaimahi' (the worker). It recognises that leaders 'lead by doing', upholding collegial practices that build capability in others in pursuit of the goals of the organisation. As well as instrumental ties (those that involve co-operation or interaction in order to achieve immediate goals and obtain tangible resources such as advice or materials), we included attention in our data collection and analysis to a range of expressive (or affective) ties – those relationships that are ends in themselves in contrast to goal-oriented relationships. We paid attention, for example, to ties that characterise those with whom respondents have a close relationship (people with whom they spend time in informal activities or candidly share personal information), from whom they receive professional encouragement (recognition of efforts and support in exploring new ideas) and those who provide an increase in positive energy after exchanges (feeling inspired, positive or motivated).

Fourthly, the leadership framework highlights the capability leaders need in attending to conditions and practices that enhance an engaging, active and achieving community that 'sees itself involved in ongoing learning, innovation and improvement for the benefit of each and all of its learners'. We also recognise the complexity of the contexts and conditions that can support and constrain relational ties, and so gathered data on a range of scales alongside social network data in order to understand the context more broadly, particularly as it relates to respondents' perceptions of peer collaboration, collective involvement, resources for collaboration and professional relationships/trust.

Finally, the framework highlights the importance of leaders' capability in 'evaluating practices' including their evaluation of both collective and individual practices in relation to learning outcomes and wellbeing. It demands that leaders use high levels of quantitative and qualitative data literacy, that they are curious about patterns and practices and that they can describe and identify problems or challenges in ways that open up real discussion and identification of needs and solutions. Our intervention was designed to help leaders demonstrate that capability by building their skill in noticing, understanding and responding to relational patterns, including problematic patterns evident in their own social network data that became the focus of action plans. We engaged them in reading network maps and learning about a range of social network measures to think about and improve social relationships across their network.

THE PROJECT CONTEXT: BETTER TOGETHER

The design of our intervention reflected that an important part of the work of curriculum leaders is to respond to challenges and opportunities that arise when giving effect to curriculum change (Sinnema & Stoll, 2020). As Sinnema and Stoll (2020) explain, they must also meet the learning demands that practitioners face when grappling with such change – these include committing to curriculum change, knowing what curriculum changes are and what they mean, understanding how to respond to curriculum changes and improving practice to realise intentions by making changes. Meeting those demands requires curriculum leaders to strengthen networks, build high trust, and activate relational ties that enable the exchange of knowledge and innovative ideas and other resources conducive to the change. Curriculum leaders need to actuate and boost social capital in support of curriculum change. Leaders are, in a sense, social/relational architects. Key assumptions we brought to the project design related to:

- **Conditions.** We should focus less on solving specific curriculum problems and more on the relational conditions conducive to curriculum realisation and improvement more generally.

- **Anticipation**. Relatedly, our efforts should support participants to strengthen the relational conditions that will have immediate benefits, but more importantly, that will see them well placed to solve as yet unknown curriculum changes inevitably coming their way in the future.

- **Strengths**. Our participants are not empty vessels needing only to be filled by our ideas about curriculum, teaching and learning. On the contrary, we recognised the diverse and expansive preexisting expertise of our participants.

- **Leverage**. Our job is to help participants realise their collective potential and learn how to leverage existing expertise lurking but potentially out of sight.

- **Pathways**. Aspirations across the system for improving how learners experience pathways through the curriculum cannot be realised without attention to the pathways of relational ties between and amongst educators in the system.

Participants – Curriculum Leaders

Our participants were some 60 curriculum leaders from two kāhui ako. The first kāhui ako, which we refer to as Pūriri, included four primary schools (three primary Y1–6 and one intermediate Y7–8) with student rolls of between 200 and 600 and a secondary school with more than 2,000 on the roll. Most of the student population in the Pūriri kāhui ako are either European (36%) or Asian (32%), and a smaller proportion of students are Māori (11%), Pasifika (7%) or other ethnicities (14%). The second kāhui ako we refer to as Mānuka; it comprised eight schools serving an ethnically diverse community. The Mānuka schools' rolls range between 100 and 700. This kāhui ako included a range of school types: three primary (Y1–6), a composite (Y1–13), two secondaries (Y9–13), one full primary (Y1–8) and an intermediate (Y7–8). Pacific students make up 60% of the student population, 23% are Asian, 15% are Māori and 1% are European.

Our project participants held a range of leadership roles including both formal and informal roles associated with their particular school (e.g. deputy principals, team leaders, heads of department, teachers in charge of a particular project) or within the kāhui ako (including across- and within-school lead teacher roles and the kāhui ako lead principals).

Intervention – Hui

The activities of the project spanned 18 months and are outlined in detail later in the book; but, by way of introduction, key activities are set out in Fig. 6.

We held an introductory hui (hui is the Māori term for a meeting or gathering) towards the end of a school year to focus on grounded stimulus. This hui grounded our project in the concepts of social capital and social network theory in a way that was engaging and accessible to curriculum leaders. The goal was to stimulate them to think of their work in a relational space and secure their commitment to a social network survey to provide rich insights into the relational space of their own network. The following school year began with both kāhui ako completing the social network survey, which they did with impressive response rates. Initial analyses of that data were shared with principals of each school in what we referred to as a 'story so far' session that was the basis for a co-design meeting involving school leaders in the planning for our subsequent activity. We then carried out guided

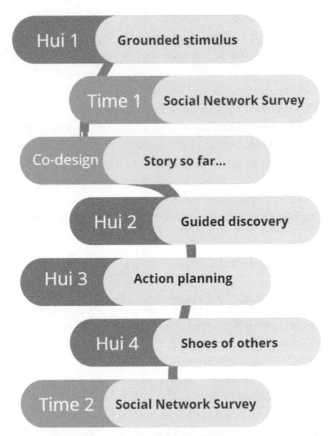

Fig. 6.   Overview of Intervention Activity.

discovery sessions with each kāhui ako, independently, in a
'Hui 2' for each. This provided a chance for curriculum leaders to delve into social network data and to consider both
strengths in the network and the problematic patterns they
agreed should be the focus of their improvement efforts.
They continued their work in schools, with some variability
according to local circumstances and because of COVID-19
restrictions and school closures. We were able to work closely

with Pūriri as they embarked on developing action plans at this stage and responding to the network insights in their kāhui ako activity. We reconvened as a group of two kāhui ako towards the end of the school year for a 'shoes of others' hui where they shared and took on each other's action plans in a step-back consultancy approach.

Central to these intervention activities and to our evaluation of their success, was data from both a social network survey and observations of leaders' practice. In the next chapter, we offer an outline of how we went about collecting and analysing that data.

5

INSIGHTS INTO THE RELATIONAL SPACE: OUR APPROACH TO DATA COLLECTION AND ANALYSIS

Relational approaches to understanding schools as social systems enable us to recognise and understand what is happening in 'the space between'. In the Better Together project, our team focussed on working with school leaders and school teams to highlight the social dynamics of their individual schools as well as in their kāhui ako. Using social network analysis (SNA) methods, we collected and analysed data that enabled our team to map the relational spaces supporting the work in curriculum team leadership. These maps provided school and system leaders with the bigger picture of the patterns of relationship within their learning communities. In this chapter, we detail our approach to data collection and analysis in order to understand the relational spaces in the Pūriri and Mānuka kāhui ako.

USING SOCIAL NETWORK ANALYSIS

The purpose of our SNA was to understand the relational structures (i.e. social networks) that underpinned the work of curriculum improvement in our two participating kāhui ako. From an intervention perspective, we wanted our analyses to provide insights that would speak to the leaders and teachers in the communities themselves. Our analyses needed to be useful in prompting action towards improvement. As such, the following questions guided our analyses:

1. What are relational patterns in these educational networks?

2. To what extent do these networks improve (i.e. strengthen) following the network intervention?

Sample

The Better Together project sought to improve the relational infrastructure across each kāhui ako; thus, the research team needed to collect data that would enable us to map the entire network (i.e. each kāhui ako) in order to develop a robust understanding of the relational patterns. To do so, all staff with any responsibility related to curriculum, teaching and learning in the Pūriri kāhui ako (comprised of four schools) and Mānuka kāhui ako (comprised of eight schools) were invited to participate. This included teachers; principals; deputy, assistant and associate principals; other senior and middle leaders; and support staff, technicians, faculty assistants, classroom assistants, guidance counsellors, librarians, ESOL co-ordinators, psychologists, learning support co-ordinators and careers advisors.

Social network research requires high survey response rates in order to reduce the extent to which missing data poses threats to validity. As Borgatti, Everett, and Johnson (2018) explain, the accuracy of measures declines with the amount of error introduced. With this in mind, and in keeping with other social network research, we considered a response rate of 75% or above

Table 3. Survey Response Rates.

	Time 1			Time 2		
	Completed	Invited	Response Rate	Completed	Invited	Response Rate
Pūriri	258	303	85%	257	291	88%
Mānuka	211	256	82%	222	272	82%

to be reliable (Borgatti, Carley, & Krackhardt, 2006; De Brún & McAuliffe, 2018). Our response rate exceeded that (Table 3).

Approach to Data Collection

The survey collected three distinct sets of data: (i) demographic data (e.g. # years of service, degree information), social network data (e.g. data on who members of the networks turn to for advice, collaboration and other relations –see Table 4) and scale data (e.g. expertise, network intentionality). Surveys were administered using an online survey solution software. The first administration, Time 1 (T1), took place at the point in time we have come to refer to as 'prepandemic' as the survey was live for 1 month at the beginning of the 2020 school year (i.e. February/March). The second administration, Time 2 (T2), took place in August/September of 2021 after the intervention activity had concluded. We refer to this data point as 'in-pandemic' because we had begun (but had not completed) administering the survey to some of the schools about three weeks prior to the announcement of further COVID-19 restrictions affecting both the Pūriri and Mānuka kāhui ako. Due to the extra demands placed on schools during this period with a (re)turn to distance learning, the process of following up with schools about response rates and sending out reminders to staff was paused for approximately 1 month.

The Bounded Approach to Social Network Survey
Design: Rosters

We designed our social network survey using a bounded
approach where all individuals identified within a predeter-
mined network boundary (i.e. each kāhui ako) were invited
to participate. This approach nicely matched our interest in
understanding the entire social system in each kāhui ako,
which was feasible given the clearly defined boundaries
(Scott, 2017) of schools and educators in these communities. Respondents were provided with a roster that listed all
of the names of all colleagues in their kāhui ako and they
were asked to nominate those with whom they have particular types of relational tie (e.g. advice). As the two kāhui ako
in our study each had more than 200 participants, which
constitutes a large network (Borgatti, Everett, Johnson, &
Agneessens, 2022), we took care to construct the survey in
a way that made it as easy as possible for the respondents to
nominate colleagues from within their school and the wider
network.

We used name organisation strategies to ease the cognitive load of respondents, given the large number of colleagues
on the roster. The list of potential colleagues with whom the
respondent might share a relationship had three main levels
of organisation. At the highest level, we divided schools into
three groups: primary, secondary and composite schools. At
the next level, we grouped potential colleagues by their particular school and then listed people in alphabetical order by
first name. This design ensured that respondents could easily
find potential colleagues from their own school, then their
own sector and then the other schools in their kāhui ako.
Ordering the lists within schools alphabetically by first name
also made it as easy as possible to locate potential kāhui ako
colleagues on the lists.

Relationships of Interest in the Social Network Survey

We focussed our survey on network relations that captured both instrumental ties (i.e. relationships such as advice and collaboration where people co-operate in order to achieve a work-related goal) and expressive ties (i.e. relationships such as encouragement that involve a commitment of some sort to the other person). Table 4 details the precise wording of the social network questions we used. In total, we collected data on seven relational dimensions, although not all dimensions were included in both surveys.

For each relation, there were two parts to the survey instruction. First, we provided a clarification for each question, offering definitions of terms to avoid differences in respondents' understanding. Second, we asked respondents to indicate either the frequency of their relationship (i.e. daily, weekly, monthly, termly, yearly) or the presence of a relationship (a binary response) by nominating those people from their kāhui ako roster with whom they had relationships.

Survey Administration

We collaborated with leaders in both kāhui ako to finalise the design and content of our surveys. We also worked closely with liaisons in each setting to ensure we had an 'on-the-ground' connection to those from whom we were seeking responses and to support the detailed work of ensuring rosters and contact information were complete and accurate. All procedures were carried out in line with the ethics approval form the University of Auckland Human Subjects Ethics Committee.

We used several approaches over and above provision of participant information as part of informed consent for ethics procedures to ensure people had a good understanding of the benefits of participating in the study both for them as an individual as well as for their kāhui ako. This was important

Table 4. Overview of Social Network Survey Questions.

Relationship Type	Survey Question for Nominating Relationships	Clarification	Survey Response Type
A. Advice	How frequently do you turn to the following people for *advice about curriculum?*	By 'curriculum', we mean: (1) the whole design and all elements used for guiding or prescribing educational aims and aspirations, (2) the beliefs about the design and elements and (3) the approaches planned to realise the aims and aspirations.	Frequency
B. Go to	Which of the following people do you typically *'go to'* for *expertise to help you address curriculum problems?*	By 'go to' we mean the people you can rely on to always follow up, provide credible and useful insights and get things done.	Binary
C. Collaborate	How frequently do you *collaborate* with the following people to *design or refine curriculum?*	By 'collaborate', we mean mutual work, sharing and exchanging ideas.	Frequency

D. Teaching and learning resources and materials	Which of the following people do you turn to for *curriculum-related resources or materials?*	By 'curriculum, teaching and learning resources and materials', we mean any tangible item you use in your practice such as resources, materials, worksheets, online tools, assessment tasks, lesson plans or rubrics.	Binary
E. Close relationship	With whom do you have a *close relationship?*	By 'close relationship', we mean a person with whom you spend time in informal activities or candidly share personal information.	Binary
F. Professional encouragement	Which of the following people provide you with *professional encouragement?*	By 'professional encouragement', we mean people who recognise your effort(s) and support you in exploring new ideas.	Binary
G. Positive energy	Which colleague(s) give you an *increase in positive energy* after an exchange?	By 'energy' we mean feeling inspired, a positive, encouraging and motivating interaction.	Binary

Note: The go to relation was only asked at T1 in the Pūriri kāhui ako. Professional encouragement was asked only at T1 for both kāhui ako while positive energy was queried only at T2 in both cases.

for maximising the response rate. We encouraged schools to allow time at a dedicated staff meeting for the survey to be completed. Providing dedicated time to complete the survey during the workday is a strategy for ensuring completion. Second, we provided a link to a video that provided an overview of the survey and explained what an analysis of respondents' network data could reveal. In addition, we provided a preparation tool – a one-page summary of the network questions – that respondents could view in advance of the online survey to orient them to the range of questions they would be asked and to provide an opportunity to reflect on relevant aspects of their networks. Throughout the data collection period, we sent out targeted survey reminders at regular intervals to those individuals who had not started or completed the survey. We also provided regular updates to the school principal and/or liaison person outlining response rates for all schools in the kāhui ako. We exceeded our minimum response rate target of 75%. This target was set because high response rates are particularly important for ensuring reliability in SNA, given that such analyses focus on understanding how everyone in a network is connected with everyone else (Borgatti et al., 2006; Kossinets, 2006).

Approaches to Data Analysis

Given that our focus in the social network analyses was on the relational patterns within and across the schools in each kāhui ako, we focussed our analysis on two levels: (i) the whole network and (ii) the individual level. At the whole-network level, we considered network cohesion measures in addition to network visualisations. Cohesion measures allow us to understand the degree of connectedness and distribution of connections among actors within a network. To take into account relationships between pairs of people, we used 'dyadic-based cohesion' measures, – depicting the overall connectedness of a network.

At the individual level, we considered various centrality measures that provide individual-level measures of network activity. Table 5 provides an explanation of each measure that was used to examine the social networks in the Pūriri and Mānuka kāhui ako. All measures were calculated using UCINet software (Borgatti, Everett, & Freeman, 2002).

Table 5.   Network Measures.

Measure	Definition
Average degree	Average degree indicates the average number of ties to and from each individual node in the network. For example, if the average degree is 4, it means that, on average, each person in the network has about four ties.
Density (D)	This measure refers to the number of ties in the network reported as a fraction of the total possible number of ties. If a network has a density of 10%, it means that out of every 10 possible ties, 1 tie is present.
Fragmentation (F)	The fragmentation measure is the opposite of connectedness. It refers to the proportion of pairs of nodes that are disconnected from each other. The higher the fragmentation number the less likely people can get to the resources of others.
Reciprocity (R)	The dyad reciprocity is the proportion of mutual ties in a network.
Degree centralisation (CD)	The degree centralisation measure indicates the distribution of average degree across a network. A highly centralised network is one in which most ties flow to or from one or very few actor(s) with the remaining actors connecting with very few ties.
Out-degree centralisation (CD_{out})	A form of degree centralisation that focusses on the extent that out-degree ties (i.e. outgoing or resource-seeking ties) flow from one or a small group of actors in a network. The higher the CD_{out} score (i.e. the closer it is to 1.0), the greater the extent to which resource-seeking behaviour focusses on a particular subset of individuals in a network.

(Continued)

Table 5.   Network Measures. (Continued)

Measure	Definition
In-degree centralisation (CD_{in})	Another form of degree centralisation that focusses on the extent that in-degree ties (i.e. incoming or resource-providing ties) flow from one or a small group of actors in a network. The higher the CD_{in} score (i.e. the closer it is to 1.0), the greater the extent to which resources provided in a network are coming from a particular subset of individuals in a network.
Average distance	Average distance refers to the average number of 'steps' (i.e. connections) it takes for an actor to reach all the potential resources within a network. For example, if the average distance is 4, it will take, on average, 4 steps to connect with everyone in the network.
Standard deviation (SD) distance	The SD of average distance refers to the range of average distance scores. If the average degree is 4 and the SD distance is 1.5, the minimum number of steps it takes to connect with everyone in the network is 2.5 and the maximum number of steps is 5.5.
Proportion (prop) within 3	Prop within 3 refers to the proportion of network actors that are accessible to ego (i.e. focal actor) within three steps. If the prop within 3 score is 0.85, it means that 85% of the actors in a network are accessible to the focal person within three steps.
Degree centrality	Degree centrality is an ego-level network measure that counts the number of ties for each individual. If an individual is connected to four others in a network, their degree centrality score is 4.0.
Out-degree centrality	Out-degree is a measure of network activity. It measures the number of times an individual *sends* a tie to another (i.e. seeks a resource from another).
In-degree centrality	In-degree is a measure of network popularity. It measures the number of times a person *receives* a tie (i.e. provides a resource to another).

Social Network Visualisations

Network visualisations (i.e. network maps) were a key tool both from an analytic perspective and in terms of informing the intervention project. Pragmatically, network maps were useful tools to spark participants' interest and as a prompt for further discussion and planning. We used NetDraw (Borgatti et al., 2002) software to generate sets of network diagrams that allowed us to visualise the pattern of interactions within each relational dimension queried (advice, go to, collaborate, materials, close professional relationship, professional encouragement and positive energy). These diagrams, or sociograms, are composed of nodes (actors) and ties (relationships). It displays how actors are related to each other through their relational linkages. We took a whole-network approach to mapping in order to capture the overall network structure. This enabled us to visualise all the ties within the network whereas an egocentric approach focusses solely on the ties surrounding a particular individual.

In addition to presenting the structural patterns of relationships, we also incorporated network measures and demographical attributes in the network sociograms to better understand the network properties including role, position and characteristics of individual actors and their connectedness. For instance, we used graphing attributes such as node size to explore depth of connectedness among individuals, colour/greyscale to indicate school clusters or perceived level of curriculum leadership efficacy, and node shape to illustrate demographic variables such as role type (e.g. school leader, teacher and so on). Fig. 7 provides an example of the network map from the Pūriri kāhui ako. Nodes are sized by in-degree, coloured by school and shaped by role. Lines indicate termly collaboration relationships.

Time 1

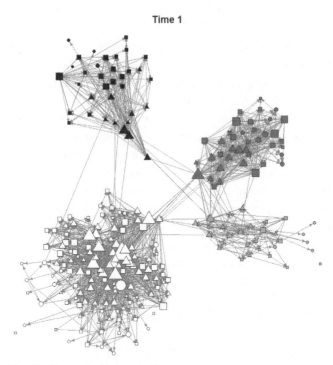

Fig. 7.   Example Network Map.
Note: In this graph, the nodes are sized by in-degree; the larger the node, the more often that person was cited as a collaboration partner. The colour of the nodes indicates the school, and the node shape corresponds to the individual's role in the school. Circles = teacher aide/support; squares = classroom teacher; triangles = formal leadership position.

Demographic and Scale Variables

Alongside the social network survey questions, we collected demographic information relating to gender, years of experience, ethnicity, positional role type, grade level, teaching area and the like. We also sought responses to scale items for eight constructs: peer collaboration, collective involvement, resources for collaboration, trust, network intentionality, team discussion quality, curriculum leadership efficacy, practice improvement and wellbeing.[1] The final section of the survey included several open-ended questions inviting respondents to reflect on the conditions that support or constrain the development of kāhui ako and areas in need of improvement.

Given that this book focusses on a social network approach to curriculum interventions, we also explored *network intentionality* – a concept that centres individuals' beliefs about their social networks and their connections with others (see Moolenaar et al., 2014). Specifically, we focussed on four dimensions: (1) network *beliefs* (the usefulness of the 'right' relationships with others), (2) network *assessment* (planning and assessing one's social networks), (3) network *connection* (favourable disposition towards connecting with others) and (4) network *activity* (actively seeking out connections with others). Networks composed of individuals who believe in the purpose and value of connection are more likely to develop and mobilise social capital (i.e. the resources available to people through their relationships with others). This scale contained 14 items. Respondents were asked to describe their level of agreement on a 6-point scale ranging from 1 (*strongly disagree*) to 6 (*strongly agree*) for each item. Our team inspected the scale data for missing data. Where less than 10% of data were missing, we imputed the missing values; however, in cases where more than 10% of the data were missing, the data were excluded. These data were included in a series of correlational analyses and hierarchical regressions; however, only the descriptive analyses are reported in this book.

CARRYING OUT OBSERVATIONS

Relying only on accounts of how people practice, regardless of how committed they are to providing a 'factual' account, is problematic; to establish a clear picture of how leaders, for example, go about leading curriculum collaborations, observations of them doing that work are invaluable. Observations also provide a shared experience between the observed and the observer that can be the basis for rich reflective dialogue.

The Purpose of Our Observations

The purpose of our observations was to gain insight into the quality of relational ties that our SNA had revealed. Network maps and measures gave us a detailed and broad-ranging picture of the relational space, much of which would be typically unobservable. Our observations served to add richness to the social network data, a chance to see for ourselves, and on behalf of our participants, how relational ties look, sound and feel in the context of their work together. From our social network approach, we had detailed network statistics and maps visualising patterns of advice relations, collaboration, sharing of resources/materials and close relationships. Our observations allowed us to see more and differently, seeing advice-seeking and giving as it happened; and to watch as collaborations were discussed, proposed or taking place. We were also able to observe in ways that captured the energy and value of close relationships and how these allowed the exchange of more work-focussed resources.

From an intervention perspective, we wanted to be able to describe the approach to leadership in a kāhui ako, so we could better support them in their role as curriculum leaders seeking to improve relationality in their networks. We observed interactions between the across school leaders (ASLs) themselves and between them and the groups of educators they led as they developed and implemented their social network action plan and addressed their achievement challenges.

We were interested in how they led change in the kāhui ako more generally and the social network improvement action plan started in Hui 2 more specifically. We wanted our observation analyses to be a tool for our intervention; describing and understanding how kāhui ako leaders carried out their roles was important not just from a research point of view, but enabled us to engage with leaders using a shared account of their actual practice, rather than generic intervention activities.

Our observations were guided by the following questions:

1. What characterises the approach to curriculum leadership of those with formal leadership roles?

2. What explains the approach to curriculum leadership of those with formal leadership roles?

3. What are the consequences of the approach to curriculum leadership of those with formal leadership roles?

Sample

Our observations were of five ASLs in Pūriri kāhui ako who we were able to visit, even amidst the disrupted year of school closures due to COVID-19. This group was given particular responsibility for progressing the social network action plan, and, as middle leaders, had a vital role in educational change and improvement (Patuawa, Robinson, Sinnema, & Zhu, 2021). We focussed on middle leaders because their work is more typically embedded in tasks than in overt attempts to motivate, engage and inspire (Robinson, 2001), and they are rarely responsible for sanctioning or rewarding others (Gaubatz & Ensminger, 2017). Rather, middle leaders lead by creating opportunities to work on improvement, structuring the tasks in which they do so and making choices about what and what not to work on. Through such tasks, group norms emerge that shape the approach taken to improvement within any particular social context.

The ASLs met as a group once a week to discuss and co-ordinate their actions. We observed five of those group meetings. In addition, each ASL led a 'working group' that included teachers from across all of the kāhui ako schools, and focussed on one of the five kāhui ako achievement challenges, including literacy, numeracy and student agency. We observed the Pūriri ASLs leading 10 half-day working-group sessions.

Approach to Data Collection

Our approach to observation drew on the approach outlined in problem-based methodology and in practitioner research as described by Robinson and Lai (2005). We observed the ASLs interacting in group meetings, observed them leading other teachers and joined in and helped where we could. In addition to observations, we regularly reflected with the ASLs after and between meetings in informal conversations. All observations were audio recorded and transcribed, and we took extensive field notes. Our observation protocol was aligned to the questions guiding our study and focussed on our goal of constructing a robust theory of action; with this in mind, we focussed, in both our observations and reflective discussions, on the ASLs' actions, constraints and consequences. Field notes served a theory-building function, intended to capture points of interest (Robinson, 1993) such as how the ASLs dealt with areas of disagreement or incoherence (e.g. between different school levels). Our aim was to record information at as low a level of inference as possible and capture our nascent theory building as we made sense of the data (e.g. see Robinson & Lai, 2005, p. 127).

Approach to Data Analysis

Our analysis was geared to constructing an accurate theory-of-action account of the ASL group's practice. From such an account, we could identify specific areas where we would be able to support them in the improvement of their social network and social network action plan. Our analysis started from identifying key actions from our observation data sets. We began by describing how the ASLs had structured their work; when, where and how often they had decided to meet; and how they had arranged to work with the other kāhui ako schools. We then looked to describe what happened within those meetings, what tasks were undertaken and how they were organised. Finally, we looked to describe how the ASLs interacted with others in their work, paying particular attention to how they reacted to any disagreement or conflict – did they engage with difference, and if so, how?

Low Levels of Inference

In constructing our account, we tried to stay at as low a level of inference as possible while remaining conscious we were generalising for a group of people. One example of how we stayed at a low level of inference can be seen in our description of the facilitators as acting 'neutrally'. From our observations of the ASLs leading their workgroups, we made the attribution that the ASLs positioned their role as one of being 'neutral' facilitators (Schwarz, 2016, p. 15). We made this attribution as the result of noticing, at several working-group sessions, that the Pūriri ASLs tended not to engage with difference when it surfaced and seldom offered their own views in discussions – even when they held strong opinions about the subject at hand.

Three specific examples we saw of facilitators adopting the neutral role stand out. The first was during a discussion on learner transitions across school levels in the literacy working group where a middle school teacher noted that they had expected students to be entering the school as 'independent readers', but that, in many cases, they were not. A little later in the discussion, a senior high school teacher noted that they expected students to be entering the high school being able to 'read to learn' but that students were often not able. The ASL chairing the session did not acknowledge the statements nor highlight their similarity, notwithstanding the criticism of the previous level of schooling implicit in the points made.

The second example of neutrality occurred during a mathematics group discussion about learner transitions between school sectors. A high school maths teacher stated that, in his opinion, it was imperative students entered the school in possession of certain 'mathematical facts'. In response, the intermediate school head of mathematics wondered aloud if by 'facts' the teacher had meant 'knowing their times-tables' and stated that he could recommend to his teachers that they rote-teach times-tables, but that, in his opinion, most of his teachers would not do so and that in any case such teaching approaches did not 'reach all kids'. Despite the focus of the session being to use precisely such information to develop learner transitions for mathematics, the Pūriri ASL leading the working group did not acknowledge the statements, nor draw any links between the expectations voiced by the teachers at different schooling levels. Rather, they moved on to the next point at hand.

The third example of remaining neutral rather than engaging with difference was observed in a working group of new entrant and Year 1 primary school teachers who were working on learner transitions to schools. The teachers were undertaking a task where they listed the skills they thought ECE students should have acquired before entering primary school. Rather than overtly leading a critique or evaluation of the suggestions made, the ASL leading the session adopted a 'leading question' approach, for example twice asking the teachers 'are these nice-to-haves or need-to-haves?' At the completion of the session, we asked for the ASL's opinion on the skills listed. She indicated that she strongly considered several to be inappropriate, but that she didn't think it was her place to say so, stating that 'no one likes a know-it-all, I don't want to be the loudest in the room'. Despite the strength of her view, she had remained neutral.

We generalised such behaviour across the ASL group as 'assume the role of neutral facilitator' and, after a working-group meeting, tested that attribution with one of the ASLs, who validated it. We then compared our theory building of the ASLs' actions when leading working groups against data of how they acted with each other in ASL meetings. We noted that they seldom engaged in disagreement either. We therefore shortened our attribution to 'act neutral' in our final account. We then presented our final account to the Pūriri ASLs, at a one-day action-planning event, who accepted it as a valid description of how they went about their work.

Our description of data collection above refers to time-points before, during and after our intervention. Next, we turn to that – the heart of our project – and introduce and explain our reasoning for the approach to our intervention overall, and the four main hui that it involved.

NOTE

1. We report on network intentionality in this book since it is central to our intervention; other measures are reported elsewhere, including, for example Cann, Sinnema, Daly, Rodway, and Liou (2022).

PART 2

BETTER TOGETHER INTERVENTION THEORY OF ACTION

In this part of the book, we use the theory of action framework introduced earlier to build a picture of our intervention approach. In Chapters 6–9, we detail the approach we took to intervention in each of four hui. But first, we provide an overarching theory of action, let's call it the 'big picture', that sets out the main thrust of all key project activities (Fig. 8).

THE BIG PICTURE

We begin our account of the big picture approach to intervention with attention to the end-goals; what were we trying to achieve? We go on to introduce other types of constraints in the constraint set in addition to the goals that, as constraints do, helped us determine what to do and what not to do. The theory of action is written from the point of view of the intervention team; it sets out our actions in relation to the constraints that explain them. The consequences of these are set out later, in Chapter 10.

The Constraints That Helped Us Design an Intervention

People's values are a key type of constraint. Of great value to our team, and to the school leaders who chose to join our project, were the people in their respective networks and the relationships amongst them. Our goal was to not only improve the network in terms of the relational ties in it but also to secure a commitment from participants to support its ongoing improvement. We were striving to create conditions conducive to curriculum realisation for the immediate and longer term. By curriculum realisation, we mean that all teaching and learning across diverse contexts reflects the values and intent of the full and complex set of curriculum elements in a deep and integrated way, leading to learners' success on the aspirations the policy sets out.

There is a myriad of ways we might have tackled those goals, so we outline next additional constraints that helped us narrow the options and devise a plan. We held a number of beliefs that helped shape our approach; we believed building commitment to and improving relational practice to be contingent on:

1) attending to the causes of existing problems,

2) developing deep understandings to make sense of and evaluate existing patterns,

3) supporting network intentionality, and

4) ensuring diversity of thought.

We knew we needed to understand the status quo, and all parties had ideas about how the networks were going, but none, at the outset, had full awareness of preexisting relational patterns. A reasonable assumption was that some of those patterns would be conducive to curriculum realisation, but

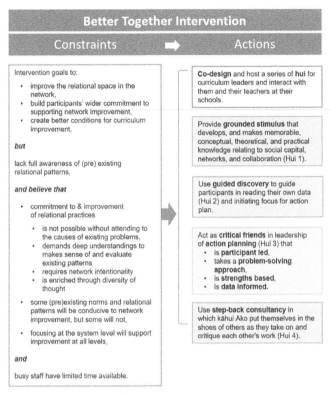

Better Together Intervention

Constraints ➡ **Actions**

Intervention goals to:

- improve the relational space in the network,
- build participants' wider commitment to supporting network improvement,
- create better conditions for curriculum improvement,

but

lack full awareness of (pre) existing relational patterns,

and believe that

- commitment to & improvement of relational practices
  - is not possible without attending to the causes of existing problems,
  - demands deep understandings to makes sense of and evaluate existing patterns
  - requires network intentionality
  - is enriched through diversity of thought
- some (pre)existing norms and relational patterns will be conducive to network improvement, but some will not,
- focusing at the system level will support improvement at all levels,

and

busy staff have limited time available.

Co-design and host a series of **hui** for curriculum leaders and interact with them and their teachers at their schools.

Provide **grounded stimulus** that develops, and makes memorable, conceptual, theoretical, and practical knowledge relating to social capital, networks, and collaboration (Hui 1).

Use **guided discovery** to guide participants in reading their own data (Hui 2) and initiating focus for action plan.

Act as **critical friends** in leadership of **action planning** (Hui 3) that
- is **participant led**,
- takes a **problem-solving approach**,
- is **strengths based**,
- is **data informed**.

Use **step-back consultancy** in which kāhui Ako put themselves in the shoes of others as they take on and critique each other's work (Hui 4).

Fig. 8. Theory of Action: Better Together Intervention.

some (and perhaps many) would not be. We also believed our system-level intervention efforts – focussing on relational ties of the whole kāhui ako system – would (or at least should) support improvement at all levels. In other words, focussing on improving relationships across the whole kāhui ako should also improve relations for each school, and subgroups within the school – syndicates, departments and the like.

These constraints led us to design an intervention comprising four hui each with distinct activities and purposes. Hui 1 was all about providing grounded stimulus – theoretical and conceptual grounding to stimulate thinking throughout the project. We focussed on theories of social capital, social networks collaboration and related concepts. Next, in Hui 2, we embarked on guided discovery – a process to engage participants with data from their social network survey – data that were from them, about them and for them. In that hui, participants identified and generated commitment to solving three problematic patterns, and elicited insights from network members about possible causes and solutions to them. In Hui 3, we worked with leaders from one kāhui ako to refine their action ensuring they could support problem solving, and be strengths based and data informed. For our final hui, a step-back consultancy approach was used: a process by which one group takes on the issues raised by the other in an effort to offer deeper insights. Kāhui ako had the opportunity to share and progress their action planning and drew on diverse perspectives of those in the other kāhui ako to do so.

Next, we elaborate on our intervention actions for each hui and the theoretical and empirical bases of the beliefs that led us to them.

6

HUI 1 – PROVIDING GROUNDED STIMULUS

In this chapter, we detail the intervention approach we took in Hui 1, a hui focussed on providing grounded stimulus (Fig. 9).

GROUNDED IN THEORY

Being 'grounded', for us, meant the intervention drew on and made a feature of robust and relevant theories; we drew on, and shared with participants, theories of social capital (Coleman, 1997) and social networks (Daly, 2010) and introduced how those theories might be used in support of curriculum realisation (Sinnema & Stoll, 2020) and to solve curriculum problems. Why did we do that? Because we knew depth would require learning, and that professional learning is supported by the integration of theory and practice. In teacher professional learning, for example, theories of curriculum, effective teaching and assessment need to be engaged with in ways that connect them to practice. These theoretical understandings, according to Timperley (2008), are useful because

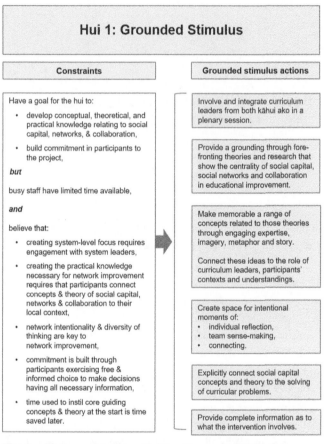

Fig. 9.   Theory of Action: Hui 1 – Grounded Stimulus.

they become 'the basis for making ongoing, principled decisions about practice in ways that flexibly meet the complex
demands of everyday teaching' (p. 11). Given our argument
that curriculum leaders have the responsibility and opportunity to foster the relational space, it follows that leadership
development too should bring theory to the table. When the
challenges leaders face in practice are complex, nuanced and

dynamic, theory becomes a steady, secure basis from which to consider possibilities and make decisions.

GROUNDED IN RESEARCH

Being grounded also meant ensuring the ideas we were exposing participants to had a strong basis in robust research. The concepts we chose to focus on (for example, reciprocity, collaboration, cohesion, etc.) and the importance we conveyed of them for the work of curriculum leaders was grounded in empirical evidence. We drew on evidence, in particular, about the relationship between the quality and nature of networks and a range of outcomes critical to the work of curriculum leaders. Sprinkled throughout our intervention activity was reference to, for example, the role of social networks in curriculum and policy implementation (Coburn & Russell, 2008; Hopkins & Spillane, 2014) and in creating innovative climates (Coburn & Russell, 2008; Frank, Zhao, Penuel, Ellefson, & Porter, 2011; Liou & Daly, 2018a; Moolenaar, Daly, & Sleegers, 2011, Moolenaar et al., 2014). We touched on the way in which networks can impact educators' capacity for data use (Farley-Ripple & Buttram, 2015), both teachers' self-efficacy and commitment (de Jong, Moolenaar, Osagie, & Phielix, 2016) and their research use (Brown, Daly, & Liou, 2016, Brown, Zhang, Xu, & Corbett, 2018). We also highlighted the importance of work on connectivity and the relational space, given empirical evidence about the impact of these on teachers' learning and improved practice (Sinnema, Liou, Daly, Cann, & Rodway, 2021), the important albeit indirect impact on student achievement (Daly, Moolenaar, Der-Martirosian, & Liou, 2014; Daly, Liou, & Der-Martirosian, 2020; Goddard, Goddard, & Tschannen-Moran, 2007; Leana & Pil, 2006; Moolenaar, Sleegers, & Daly, 2012; Ronfeldt, Farmer, McQueen, & Grissom, 2015).

STIMULUS

The idea of theory and evidence as a 'stimulus' led us to two important considerations. First, theory was a stimulus in the sense that it wasn't enough on its own; it had to stimulate something. Whenever theory was being referred to, we sought to make clear (a) its general relevance to practice and (b) our expectations that participants would employ the theory in their own practice in particular and unique ways. Second, theory being a stimulus required it to be presented in a stimulating and memorable way – to shake perceptions of 'dreary theory'! For this, we used a cognitively and emotionally engaging approach to introduce the relevant theories and support the theory/practice connections to be made. The session was concept rich; a wide array of concepts related to the key theories were introduced. For most, these theories and concepts were either familiar, at best, or entirely new and intriguing. This new learning, experienced as a collective, gave participants a shared language to use in talking about their network together, and a robust basis for evaluating the quality of their existing relational space. For the session to act as a stimulus, it needed to be memorable and engaging. With this in mind, theories and concepts were introduced with the use of images, metaphor and story (both personal and derived from research), using contexts from both within and beyond education.

STIMULUS THROUGH METAPHOR

Metaphor was used to engage participants with key ideas, and to ensure they were memorable. Take, for example, the concept of reciprocity. Using an account of how monkeys' social interactions influence their grooming of each other, the point was made that past social interactions are influential in determining future interactions. As Majolo, Schino, and Aureli (2012) found, in their study of reciprocity during grooming exchanges in long tailed macaques, whether a monkey groomed another, and for how long they groomed the other monkey, predicted the latency and occurrence of grooming in return – direct reciprocity. Does knowing about monkeys' grooming matter to curriculum leaders? Probably not. Does remembering the importance of reciprocity matter for curriculum leaders? Definitely, and metaphors are a powerful tool to support that meaning-making. As the work of Thibodeau and Boroditsky (2011) shows, metaphors have a powerful influence over how people go about solving problems; they influence in profound ways how we conceptualise and act on important issues. They can explain our perspectives on the world: 'how we think about things, make sense of reality, and set the problems we later try to solve' (Schön, 1979, p. 137).

The monkey grooming metaphor was used to anchor the understanding that reciprocity for humans is, just as it is for some primates, crucial in our social world. We are much more likely to provide care, or support, or resources for others, if they have done so for us. And, on the flip side, we are much more likely to feel comfortable approaching someone for support or resources if we have previously provided for them. Such reciprocated relationships are critical for vulnerability and trust to flourish.

Metaphor was also used to convey the point about systems of care and nurture and exchange being hidden in plain sight, but vital to the wellbeing of collectives. The compelling example of the 'wood-wide web' was shared, which explains how trees interact with one another in networks; they are intricately connected, exchanging information and resources through fungi (Helgason, Daniell, Husband, Fitter, & Young, 1998). These metaphors opened up the space for consideration and freedom to explore important ideas from different perspectives.

STIMULUS THROUGH METAPHOR COMBINED WITH IMAGERY

Images were used together with metaphor to make important concepts memorable. Four key ideas about levers of ideation rate, for example, were introduced with carefully chosen bold imagery. The value of more participants for ideation was shown through contrasting a single hand-drawn symbol of an idea (a light bulb) with a gathering of multiple light bulbs. The importance of diversity of perspectives was conveyed through a close-up photograph of a range of spices different in colour, texture and (of course) taste, collected together, vibrant and bold. The idea about the importance of increased frequency of ideas was conveyed with an image of multiple fern fronds alongside each other. The idea about engaging with ideas was expressed through a bird's-eye-view photograph of a sailing boat – the wind hitting the sails and taking the boat forward.

To make the contrast between connection and isolation memorable, an image of van Gogh's work – *The Yellow House* – was shown, and the story told of van Gogh writing to his brother, excited about creating an artists' colony; bringing artists together to create. The image loomed large as participants heard the quote from van Gogh, 'You know I've always thought it ridiculous for painters to live alone. You always lose when you're isolated'. The metaphor was meaningful in positioning our curriculum leaders also as designers and creators who should be connected, not separated, opening up new ways of considering roles.

One of our goals was to make these metaphors and the many new concepts memorable, and thoughtful use of images made sense for this purpose. We know from decades of empirical work on memory and cognition that pictures not only deepen understandings but are also remembered better and for longer than ideas presented in other modes. There is convincing evidence, as summarised by McBride and Dosher (2002), for what is known as the 'picture superiority effect': 'increased memory performance for picture stimuli over word stimuli has been found in countless studies of recall and recognition... there is no question that picture superiority exists under many conditions' (p. 424).

Some of the earliest experiments in this field, from the work of Paivio and Csapo (1973), involved participants studying pictures, concrete words and abstract words under a range of conditions. Later, tests showed better recall of pictures than either type of word. Similarly, in Shepard's (1967) experimental studies using recognition memory trials, testing subjects' recall of words, sentences and images, images were found to be much more easily recalled than words or sentences.

Why might images be so memorable? Why pictorial superiority? Ensor, Bancroft, and Hockley (2019) outline two possible explanations – one focusses on dual-coding theory (Paivio, 1991). The theory goes that we have two independent memory pathways – one stores verbal representations (the logogen pathway) and the other stores imaginal representations (the imagen pathway). Connections can be made between the pathways, so when we store an image of say a flock of starlings in murmuration in one place, an interconnection can be made to the word 'murmuration' in the other. That interconnection is more likely than the converse – We are unlikely to hear the word murmuration and create for ourselves an associated image to store. The dual-coding that occurs when we encounter an image makes us more likely to be able to access that idea later.

The second explanation for the pictorial superiority effect, as Ensor et al. (2019) explain, is distinctiveness. Distinctiveness might be physical in nature, and so memory for pictures occurs because pictures vary more in their physical features than words. Put otherwise, the word murmuration is more similar to all other words than the picture of starlings in murmuration is to all other pictures. Distinctiveness can also be conceptual in nature, with deeper levels of processing involved in identifying a picture than words.

Further support for our emphasis on images in our hui comes from the work of Whitehouse, Maybery, and Durkin (2006) in relation to the picture superiority effect. While not a study of adults, they did find that the magnitude of the effect increases with age from younger children through to adolescents. This is probably due to increased inner speech being available the older one gets and so the likelihood of encoding a pictorial stimulus in both pathways is greater, making it easier to access in memory.

Moving Imagery

Metaphors were cemented not only through still imagery but also through the presentation of moving imagery. The concept of murmuration, for example, was introduced using vivid and mesmerising video footage of murmurating starlings accompanied by moving classical music. Murmuration is the synchronous movement in groups towards a collective goal; in starlings, we see this in large numbers of birds, before sunset, performing amazing aerial manoeuvres before they settle down and roost for the night, as Ballerini et al. (2008) put it, 'swirling with extraordinary spatial coherence' (p. 201). Famous studies of starlings in murmuration have given insight into their ability to manage uncertainty well, when seeking to maintain consensus, and how that is influenced by who is interacting with whom (Young, Scardovi, Cavagna, Giardina, & Leonard, 2013). The work of Young et al. (2013) involved collecting many photographs of starlings in flight, and using mathematical models to understand the cohesiveness of relationships between neighbouring birds. Even though the starling flock is exposed to much uncertainty, and disturbances in the environment (just like educators face), and has little vocal exchange (less typical of educational contexts), the flocks were found to maintain coherence and cohesion because they follow certain rules. Each bird:

- pays attention to six to seven of its nearest neighbours,

- flies towards those neighbours but without crowding,

- turns with neighbours if any of them turn.

These principles of alignment, separation, cohesion and of correcting and sustaining course in the world of starlings, have important parallels for curriculum leaders seeking to foster cohesiveness in educational networks. This part of the presentation prompted curriculum leaders to think about their 'neighbours', how they might work with them without overcrowding and the way in which educational turns might be taken together. It was, they told us, very memorable.

Stimulus Through Story (Research Told as Story/ Personal Story)

To convey the importance of nurturing social capital, and the point that group success is contingent on social connectedness, William Muir's (2005) research with chickens was used. Muir's experiment involved separating chickens that were average in terms of egg production and those he referred to as 'super chickens' (i.e. those that were prolific egg layers). He kept them apart, in their respective groups, for multiple generations. At the conclusion of the study, he found the average chickens to be doing well – they had produced consistently. The super chickens? Not so much. Most had been pecked to death, and only three super chickens had survived. Competition amongst them, rather than collaboration, had led to aggression, dysfunction, hoarding of resources and waste.

Rather than share research with participants using a dry descriptive account, our team took a classic storytelling approach. We turn to the work of Egan (1998) to think about why storytelling is so powerful. Using the example of planning for children's learning, he highlights how typical approaches to planning (moving through a sequence of objectives, content, methods and evaluation) tend to neglect the importance of meaning in teaching and learning. He argues convincingly for the story form as a valuable approach that supports the grasp of deep meanings. And we would argue its value in our work with curriculum leaders too.

Through storytelling, the researcher was positioned as a character ('so there was a guy called William Muir, and one day he decided…'), dialogue was used to convey research procedures and findings ('and so he said, I'm gonna…') and the sequence of research events was conveyed as an unfolding plot ('and what do you know, after four generations had passed…'). In line with important characteristics of good story telling (Egan, 1998), binary opposites were introduced (the group of super chickens and the group of average chickens) and dramatic content articulated those binaries (especially the drama of the super chickens killing each other). The vivid nature of our storytelling approach made memorable the important ideas from Muir's (2005) work with chickens and other human evidence about the need for cohesion, social sensitivity and turn-taking for successful groups (Woolley, Chabris, Pentland, Hashmi, & Malone, 2010). Other storytelling in this hui touched on more personal stories that revealed the power of connection, and stories of the responses to social movements in history that remind us of the importance of connectivity.

STIMULATING THROUGH INTENTIONAL MOMENTS

Throughout the hui, there were intentional moments for individual reflection, team sense-making and connection between participants. These moments were intentional in two ways. First, they were carefully considered and designed to happen; and second, they prompted network intentionality. They explicitly, and in some cases implicitly, prompted participants to consider what they might do differently in their networks, the ties they might seek out or create, the things they might say or do with and for others, and the role they might play in building social capital. In relation to the point about incorporating diverse perspectives, for example, participants were asked to reflect with these prompts:

• In what ways do you explicitly engage diverse perspectives and alternative viewpoints in your school/kāhui ako/unit/ team?

• How do you build deep and diverse relationships?

• How might you provide more opportunities for a diversity of perspectives to enable innovation and inform decision making?

And similarly, in relation to the concepts of vulnerability and reciprocity, they took a moment to reflect on these questions:

- To what degree does *vulnerability* and *reciprocity* thrive in your school/network/unit/team?

- How might *you* create more opportunities to build high-trust interactions?

These intentional moments reflect the importance we attribute to structured reflection in teacher professional learning (Korthagen, 2001). At times, reflective moments created space for cognitive dissonance (Festinger, 1957; Mills & Harmon-Jones, 1999) – the surfacing of a realisation that attitudes, beliefs and/or behaviours might be conflicting, demanding the alteration of one of those.

As well as individual reflection, the prompts were the focus of team reflection. Sense-making, which Weick (1995) explains as structuring the unknown in order to be able to act, was an important part of our process. Opportunities to do that sense-making in teams during the hui were important given the properties of sense-making (Weick, 1995) and, in particular, its social property, as we hear in the words of Ashmos and Nathan (2002):

> *We make sense of things in organizations while in conversation with others, while reading communications from others, and while exchanging ideas with others. Others are integral to our efforts to make sense of things because what we say or think or do is contingent on what they say and think and do. Even if we are alone, we imagine the response of others to our actions or thoughts, and*

adjust our thinking and behavior accordingly. Sense-making requires talking, interaction, conversation, argument and dialogue with others. (p. 204)

Importantly, the intentional moments demanded connection – an opportunity for curriculum leaders who often did not have time to talk, let alone talk about their network, to be connected and share ideas.

7

HUI 2 – USING GUIDED DISCOVERY

In this chapter, we detail the intervention approach we took in Hui 2, a hui focussed on guided discovery (Fig. 10).

DISCOVERY

Hui 2 took a discovery orientation. We had already carried out and analysed data from a social network survey in each kāhui ako. Our findings became data for our participants – they were gifted an array of resources: a set of 24 of their network maps and a summary of their network statistics. There was much for our participants to discover and learn from. In the words of Bruner (1961), discovery is

> *a necessary condition for learning the variety of techniques of problem solving, of transforming information for better use, indeed for learning how to go about the very task of learning. Practice in discovering for oneself teaches one to acquire*

information in a way that makes that information
more readily viable in problem solving. (p. 4)

Our approach departed from the individualist approach implied in Bruner's 'oneself'; we saw discovery as a collaborative activity gathering participants around the data to grapple together with its meaning and shared implications. We like Bruner's idea that 'discovery, like surprise, favors the well prepared mind' (p. 21) – and so our hui began by revisiting

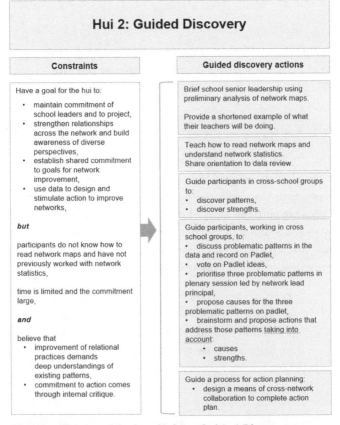

Fig. 10.   Theory of Action: Hui 2 – Guided Discovery.

key concepts introduced in Hui 1, which prepared our participants with a way of thinking about the data in front of them.

GUIDED DISCOVERY

Mindful of long-standing critiques of pure discovery approaches in compulsory education (Ausubel, 1962), including that it doesn't make sense to expect people to discover anew everything which has already been discovered by others before them, our approach emphasised the *guided* aspect of guided discovery. It was somewhat structured through the use of prompts and focussed on goals as Mayer (2004), and earlier proponents of guided discovery before him (e.g. Gagné & Brown, 1961), argues guided discovery for learners should be. We prompted them:

- to focus on description, not judgement; no shame, no blame!

- to generate one to two descriptions for each map, resisting the urge to jump to interpretation; and then to look for overall patterns across the maps

- to look for big ideas that might be leveraged to make the network stronger

- to think at a systems level, to focus on the overall CoL, not individual schools or individual educators

- to discuss what they were noticing with others

- to record both strengths and patterns on a Padlet (a digital canvas for sharing ideas).

The guided nature of the discovery hui was also appropriate given the level of prior experience our participants had with the concepts and data we were offering them to engage with. We knew social network theory and social network maps were relevant and welcomed terrain, but it was also *new* terrain for our participants – on the whole, they were unfamiliar with how to go about reading surface and/ or nuanced meanings from social network maps, or how to interpret both basic and more sophisticated statistical network measures. We were also mindful of evidence about the role of incremental scaffolds in guiding discovery in these situations. For example, in the study of students learning in biology, Großmann and Wilde's work (2019) shows that when students have low prior knowledge, using incremental scaffolds during guided discovery helps lead them to higher conceptual and procedural knowledge than when they are provided with fully worked out examples.

AN INCREMENTAL APPROACH

With this kind of incremental approach in mind, we first introduced just two key ideas – that network maps show nodes that represent actors or individuals in schools (and these were coloured by school), and that lines on the map represent ties or relationships between actors. These ideas were initially applied to the reading of one map – a map showing patterns of advice-seeking. Next, we introduced the idea that maps can vary in what their analysis focusses on – and that the set of maps not only comprised those about a range of different relationship types (advice, collaboration, materials, close relationships, etc.) but also representing different frequencies of relationship (we used monthly and yearly maps). Then we introduced four measures: density, reciprocity, average degree and fragmentation, and guided participants to notice statistics about these measures on the maps. The map-reading tool was provided for them to return to as needed (see Table 6).

CONTRASTING CASES

Once participants were showing confidence in using the concepts described above, they were guided to engage in comparing maps of different types. They began asking about contrasts between networks, for example:

- How do patterns of advice relationships compare to those for collaboration?

- How do patterns of instrumental ties (e.g. advice, materials, collaboration) compare to expressive ties (close relationships, encouragement or energy, for example)?

- How do patterns vary when we compare networks at different levels of frequency – for example, monthly advice ties compared to yearly advice ties?

- What do comparisons of in-degree and out-degree for the same networks suggest we should pay attention to?

Similarly, they asked about contrasts between those in particular roles:

- How are leaders positioned in the network, in comparison to how teachers tend to be positioned?

- How are we, as a group of Better Together project participants, positioned in relation to others?

Steering attention to comparisons in this way is a strategy that picked up on what we know about the power of contrasting cases. In the context of understanding texts, Schwartz and Bransford's (1998) work reveals how analysing contrasting

Table 6. Map-Reading Tool.

	Definition	How to read it
Node	Represents individuals by schools, individuals are referred to as 'actors'. Nodes are coloured by school	Colour: School Sized: by 'In-degree' (the number of incoming ties an actor receives from other actors.) The larger the node, the more often the actor is selected by others Position: Actors with more in/out ties are more centrally located

Line	Represents a 'tie' (relationship) between 'actors'	Direction of arrows:
		
		    Sending (out)
		    Receiving (in)
		    Reciprocal (mutual)

Density	The proportion (percentage) of: existing ties in the network possible ties in the network	A higher percentage indicates a greater number of ties within the network. The percentage allows comparisons across different relationships
Reciprocity	The proportion (percentage) of: existing mutual ties in the network possible mutual ties in the network	A higher percentage indicates the greater number of mutual ties within the network. The percentage allows comparisons across different relationships
Average degree	The number of ties the average actor has to others	A higher number indicates that the average actor is connected to a greater number of others
Fragmentation	The proportion of pairs of ties that are unreachable	A higher fragmentation indicates that the network is less connected with a greater percentage of actors who cannot reach each other

cases supports students' learning. The contrasts in cases, they argue, allows specific features that differentiate phenomena to be discerned and deeper understandings of important principles to be established. We would argue that contrasting cases are equally useful to support curriculum leaders in discerning important features of phenomena related to social systems, as portrayed in network maps. The contrasts under comparison, outlined above, allowed our participants deeper understandings about the social space they are a part of than would otherwise be possible, and led to deeper consideration of important patterns. For example,

- differences between in-degree and out-degree for the collaboration network provoked discussion about the possibility of variable understandings about what constitutes collaboration

- comparing maps showing the whole network (that indicated some level of across-school collaboration), and maps showing just project participants (orange nodes), was confronting in a motivating way given it suggested the people in the room were not part of across-school ties to the extent they might have wanted to be

- comparing network statistics for instrumental relationships (materials) and expressive relationships (encouragement) led to rich discussion regarding whether more existing expressive ties could be activated for instrumental purposes.

PROBLEM SOLVING

The first part of our guided-discovery hui was, for our leaders, an information gathering exercise. We then worked through a quite structured approach to problem solving, (a) to identify and agree on three problematic patterns to be the focus of

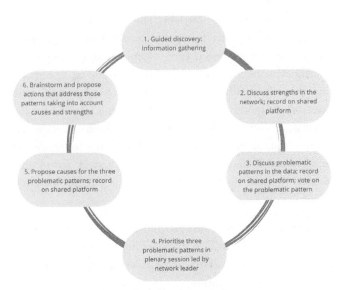

Fig. 11. The Problem-Solving Approach.

the leaders' efforts, (b) to surface possible causes for those problematic patterns and (c) to begin brainstorming possible solutions to the problems that are logically aligned to the problems' causes and strengths in the network. Our process is detailed in Fig. 11.

We took a quite structured approach because problems like these are complex and ill-structured; structured response is more likely, in this scenario, than intuitive approaches to be successful. A structured approach also made sense because problem solving is hard, because educational leaders vary in the capabilities in this area, and because problem causes are too rarely engaged with in problem-solving efforts. The approach involved the following:

1. Information Gathering. Information gathering is important in problem solving because, as Mumford, Higgs, Todd, and Elliott (2019) explain, it is a way of making sense of the environment to reduce uncertainty and increase the chance of success. Uncertainty is an important consideration in problem solving (Caughron, Ristow, & Antes, 2019); it is important given the motivating role it has in sense-making, and the need for it to be reduced in order for solutions to be developed. Uncertainty is also high in problem contexts involving entire social systems – they are by their very nature highly complex, that is they have variables with high levels of interdependence (Halbesleben, Novicevic, Harvey, & Buckley, 2003) and leaders' interaction in that environment alters it in the process (Caughron et al., 2019). The maps and statistics we provided helped to reduce uncertainty and make sense of complexity for our leaders by summarising data on 10s of 1,000s of possible relational ties in a single map on a single page, and presenting a set of such maps for them to explore. As Fig. 12 shows, the maps stimulated many ideas and theories amongst our participants.

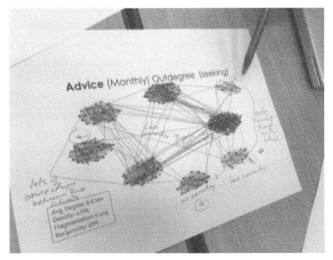

Fig. 12.   Exploration of Maps.

In problem solving, there is a tendency for leaders to turn to those with whom they already have strong ties for information about the problem. In our project, the beauty of providing our kāhui ako with the 'map/stat set' was that it made sure everyone took account of information from those with whom they had weak ties (Granovetter, 1973, 1983). By its very nature (and given the high response rates we achieved), our social network survey provided curriculum leaders with information derived from a much wider range of sources than they could possibly have achieved using their usual processes of information gathering. It reduced potential bias in leaders' perception of how their network was functioning and gave them a much fuller and richer picture of their network than they had ever seen before. And that picture surfaced problematic patterns to which they were inspired to respond.

2. Strengths. We considered the notion of problems in the most positive sense – gaps between a current state and more desired state – our process of establishing that gap was positive in that it created shared commitment to a common goal for our curriculum leaders to work on. It was also positive problem solving in the sense that we drew attention to strengths to be drawn on – either individual and collective strengths from a human-capital point of view, or strengths from a social-capital point of view – network patterns that were already as one would like.

3. Problematic Patterns Identifying and Voting. Working together, our curriculum leaders all had the opportunity to share, on the Padlet, their perspective on problematic system-level patterns they had seen in the network maps. Using the voting function, they identified problems that were most deserving of attention.

4. Problematic Pattern Prioritising. The kāhui ako leaders were then engaged to facilitate a session to prioritise three problematic patterns to focus on in an improvement action plan. We had sorted and ranked the various patterns shared on Padlet according to the voting, to support their facilitation. Turning this part of the session over to the participants' own leaders was an important part of the process; it signalled that we, as interventionists, were not the source of answers, but this was the work of the network, for themselves, with our support.

The strengths, problematic patterns are summarised in Table 7.

Table 7.   Strengths and Problematic Patterns Identified by Participants.

The Pūriri kāhui ako	The Mānuka kāhui ako
Key strengths:	Key strengths:
• In the collaboration network: good connections inside schools • Better Together team has strong reciprocal relationships • Distributed leadership evident	• Strong ties within schools • Good levels of reciprocity in advice, go to and materials networks
Problematic patterns:	Problematic patterns:
• Not enough opportunities for collaboration across schools • Not enough sharing of expertise • Currently not as much reciprocity across schools as we would like	• Fewer across- than within-school ties • Leadership ties need strengthening across the CoL • Fewer collaboration ties than advice

5. Problem Causes. Next, we asked our curriculum leaders to suggest explanations for the problematic patterns and enter them into a second Padlet. We asked them to do this individually (and anonymously if they wished) so that all possible explanations could be considered, including those that may have been risky for participants to share publicly. We wanted a full and honest account of why some of the less ideal relational patterns might be happening.

Why did we focus on problem causes? There is good evidence to suggest that attention to causal analysis results in 'higher quality, more original, and more elegant problem solutions' (Mumford et al., 2019, p. 127). As such, analysis of problems is a key skill for leaders; they dictate the actions that will be taken and help ensure that problem solutions are well aligned to problem cause. For this reason, our process in this hui created space explicitly for exploring problem cause. We realised that what leaders assume to be causing problems provides a foundation for the structure of mental models they use to understand those problems (Strange & Mumford, 2005). So we were keen to ensure that a diverse array of perspectives was brought to bear on the groups' understanding of potential causes.

Our prompt to engage in causal analysis led to a range of reasons for problematic patterns being surfaced (see, e.g. Table 8).

To finish the hui, session leaders were alerted to the next step in the process – to devise an action plan addressing the patterns, explanations and proposed actions in Padlet 2, and to discuss how they would go about implementing it. The various COVID-19 lockdown circumstances meant that one kāhui ako was able to progress their action plan prior to the next hui and the other came to the next hui ready to begin their action plan at that time.

Table 8. Proposed Causes of Problematic Patterns.

Problematic Pattern	Examples of Suggested Causes	Examples of Suggested Solutions
Not enough opportunities for collaboration	• We might not see the common purpose • People are used to working in their 'bubbles' or silos or schools and may not feel comfortable shifting from this • The purpose of the collaboration needs to be of value to all parties involved – the benefits need to outweigh the costs	• More deliberately set times for collaboration • Change infrastructure to support collaboration • Have across-school meet-ups to discuss common goals or expectations (literacy, numeracy) • Set up opportunities for teachers to observe in other schools
Not enough sharing of expertise	• People might not see themselves as an expert. A barrier can be a tendency to be humble. It is also knowing who to go to • Habit – people already have their 'go to' when looking for help, ideas or expertise • Lack of knowledge of others' expertise – we do not know what expertise each other has to be shared....	• Making kāhui ako goals clear to all • Online tools to talk • Sharing what we do and student successes with others – invitations to local schools • Schools working together to plan sports/ cultural events for our community • Reinvigorate and utilise the kāhui ako website
Fewer across-school than within-school ties	• Not knowing who. Not knowing contexts. Not knowing timetables. Relationships not established. Time • Competition between schools • Historical issues of trust • Within school is a safer place – more comfortable to seek/collaborate with people who know us and our context	• Start with small collaborative tasks. Small professional learning groups based around need or interest of challenge • Create some type of register of expertise • Kāhui ako teams set up regular meetings to develop stronger relationships

8

HUI 3 – A PROBLEM-SOLVING APPROACH TO ACTION PLANNING

In this chapter, we detail the intervention approach we took in Hui 3, a hui focussed on being critical friends in an action planning session (Fig. 13).

Our intervention was able to include, for Pūriri kāhui ako, a day dedicated to working with the across school leads (ASLs) on their action plan where we adopted the role of critical friends. The spur for the action planning day was our observations of the ASLs' leadership of improvement within the kāhui ako, as outlined in the section on observation in Chapter 5. We worked alongside the ASLs observing and reflecting together on both their meetings as a leadership team and in the working groups they were each facilitating. Our team noted that although the groups were progressing towards their curricular aims, their progress on the social network improvement action plan was slower. We also noticed that certain aspects of their leadership practice had made achieving their curricular goals more difficult. For example,

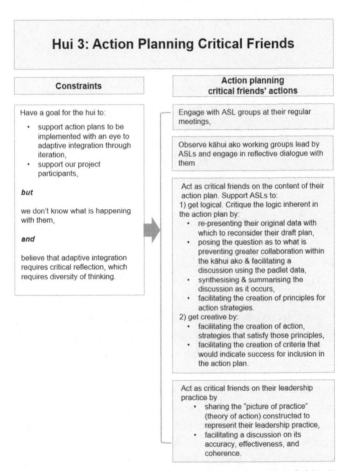

Fig. 13.   Theory of Action: Hui 3 – Action Planning Critical Friends.

their positioning of themselves as neutral facilitators had, on occasion, prevented them from being able to engage participants in discussing information directly relevant and vital to the resolution of their curricular aims. Therefore, we planned a one-day session where we could facilitate progress on their action plan and present what we noticed about their leadership for their critical reflection.

CRITICAL FRIENDS ON THE CONTENT OF THEIR ACTION PLAN

The action planning day began with a reminder that the social network action plan was intended to support problem solving to improve their three problematic patterns with the ultimate aim of seeing their curriculum foci progressed – improving curriculum, teaching and learning relating to numeracy, literacy, science, wellbeing and agency. Using a summary diagram (Fig. 14), we began the day by reemphasising that our participants' curriculum, teaching and learning goals were inextricably linked to them making progress on their goal for improved collaboration. Similarly, improving collaboration required that they have meaningful tasks on which to collaborate.

There were two key thrusts to our support of their action plan development: getting logical and getting creative.

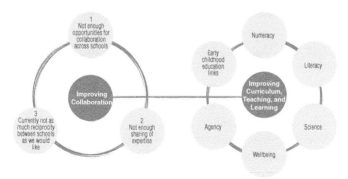

Fig. 14. Improvement Goal Dependency.

GETTING LOGICAL

We turned the ASL team's attention to closely examining their draft social network action plan and questioning its logic. We wanted them to consider if the actions were likely to solve the problematic patterns they had identified and were committed to improving. The focus was on ensuring any actions were explicitly connected with the causes of the problematic patterns. We re-presented the original data that had been used to create the draft plan. This data included the original social network maps and Padlets. We then prompted a discussion in which the ASLs combed the data for insights that would help ensure there was a solid logic to their action plan, so that it clearly addressed the underlying reasons for the problematic patterns. To guide the discussion, we posed the question, 'what is preventing greater collaboration across the kāhui ako?' to the ASLs and encouraged them to take a more 'helicopter' view of the data in answering it.

The ASLs delved into the data, highlighting and colour-coding the various causes their fellow network members had proposed and grouping them thematically. The causes had typically been phrased in the negative. As the discussion progressed, we synthesised the emerging themes and reframed them as positives to form a set of six key problem constraints that would have to be satisfied for their action plan to be effective. Each of these constraints was logically linked to multiple entries on the Padlet, from their colleagues, about what might explain the problematic pattern: Each of these constraints was logically linked to multiple comments on the Padlet from their colleagues (explanations of the problematic pattern). Following the conversation, the ASLs identified five general action strategies specifically designed to satisfy the six constraints (Table 9).

Table 9. Logical Development of Constraints to Guide New Actions.

Comments	Problem Explanations to Address	Constraints – the Action Plan Should:	Action Strategies
• 'Clarify what expertise we are wanting, is it just curriculum expertise or more broad expertise?' • 'When have we had an opportunity to share and identify our expertise? Will people raise their hand? Will we recognise our abilities and those of others?'	• A lack of awareness of each other's expert knowledge is a barrier to collaboration across our schools	**Knowledge** • answer questions about what was meant by knowledge or expertise, would have to take into account who had it, ask if it was available and how to leverage it if not, and if student voice should be included	1. Build awareness of existing expertise 2. Support those who are humble about their own expertise to make it known 3. Highlight the relevant expertise across sectors and contexts
• 'Busyness of schools and roles can make people hesitant to ask more of people' • 'Allocation of space—time where it's (a) needed the most and (b) doesn't impact negatively on our teaching responsibilities'	• Time and availability limit opportunities for collaboration	**Feasibility** • fit existing time, routine and resource constraints	4. Recognise and value the sharing of expertise 5. Break habits of typical 'go to' colleagues.
• 'Knowing the purpose of meeting together, is it time to develop creative problem solving or be transactional?' • 'Lack of purposeful opportunity. We don't know what we don't know'	• People may not understand the purpose of collaboration	**Purpose** • be purposeful and of value to people, establish shared priorities and deal with important – as opposed to urgent – problems, and consider whether the purpose was to just share or delve deeper	

(Continued)

Table 9. Logical Development of Constraints to Guide New Actions. (Continued)

Comments	Problem Explanations to Address	Constraints – the Action Plan Should:	Action Strategies
• 'People are used to working in their "bubbles" or silos or schools and may not feel comfortable shifting from this' • 'People already have their "go to" when looking for help/ideas/expertise'	• We operate in silos	**Behaviour** • the plan would have to address how to change existing habitual ways of working, for example breaking out of historical silos	
• 'Do we seek advice to "fix" rather than take the time to enter into a reciprocal conversation where we can build and develop an ongoing relationship?' • 'We don't yet have the relational trust to communicate openly'	• We recognise the relational aspect of our work is important	**Relationships** • the plan would have to answer questions about knowing each other, trust, valuing expertise, issues of judgemental behaviour and ways of working together	
• 'People may have perceived risk around the outcomes of seeking out advice or sharing their ideas'; 'people not wanting to impose on others' time'	• Emotional risk is a possible barrier to collaboration	**Emotions** • the plan would need to ensure people felt safe by ensuring risks were managed	

GETTING CREATIVE

We then asked the ASLs to get creative and brainstorm concrete and creative actions for their generic action strategies. They were asked to reexamine existing ideas for action, ensuring they satisfied the six constraints and changing them where they did not. They were also asked to generate new ideas for action that also satisfied the constraints. Examples of their concrete actions were:

- 'Expert snapshots': create a regular slot in staff newsletters from within and beyond their own school; 'Video extravaganza': have teachers create a video presenting, for example, their teaching as an inquiry area, or a lesson.

- 'Expertise matchmaking': connecting people seeking with those who have expertise, facilitated by the ASLs; 'share and send': 'here you go – let me introduce you to …'

- 'Fly on the wall' and 'meeting crasher': inviting teachers from other schools to attend school events in other schools as an observer, or to attend and possibly present at staff or year level/subject area meetings in other schools.

Next, we asked them to consider criteria that would indicate success for any of the actions and to include such indicators in their action plan. The action plan session was then set aside for the final part of the session.

CRITICAL FRIENDS ON LEADERSHIP PRACTICE

Our critical friendship extended next to supporting the ASLs' leadership of the action plan. Our prior observations of them working together as a leadership team and facilitating their respective working groups had provided us a great deal of data on their leadership approach/es. We had used the data gathered to construct a theory of action map describing their leadership in what we referred to as a picture of practice. This session was an opportunity for us to share our theory of action map, gain insight into its accuracy, and to further understand the constraints that explained their practice. We hoped that by presenting our theory of action for their reflection we would enable them to consider taking up alternative approaches to leadership that might better achieve their twin curricular and social network improvement goals.

The Picture of Practice (Figure 15) described three main leadership practices: turn-taking, establishing joint work and

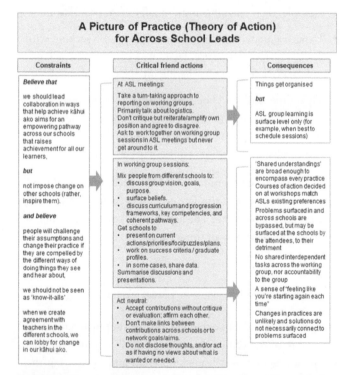

Fig. 15. Theory of Action: Hui 3 – A Picture of Practice for Across-School Leads.

acting neutral. We noticed amongst this group a tendency for *turn-taking* – rotating the schools at which their meetings were held and having small groups of teachers, mixed from different schools, take turns at sharing during working groups.

Another tendency was to focus working groups on *establishing joint work*. We identified shared interests or concerns that would be fruitful to work on together and would demand the expertise of those from different schools. For example, they focussed on developing clarity about curriculum-level expectations across learners' transitions between schools. Their conversations surfaced comparisons about how primary and middle school colleagues pitched expectations for their respective levels of the curriculum. Similarly, they talked about their respective understandings of progression in literacy across primary, middle and secondary school curriculum levels, and tools for assessing learner agency across the year levels. They focussed on problems of practice that specifically required collaboration across schools in order to really dig into those problems and move towards solutions.

While we acknowledged these productive practices, we turned our focus to a more problematic aspect of their leadership approach that we had noticed. Recalling that ASLs tended to remain neutral, adopting the role of neutral facilitator when chairing working groups questioned the reasons why, and challenged the reasons where appropriate. For example, ASLs felt that relationships were not good enough to engage with disagreements in public working group meetings. Their rationale was that relationships had to be worked on first, and then disagreements could be addressed. The intervention team challenged this belief, pointing out that engaging with difference – if done well – has the potential to build strong and respectful relationships, and in a much shorter time. There is empirical support for this claim both from within education and beyond. Silver and Shaw, (2022), for example, study the impact of people 'taking sides' or 'staying out of it' in relation to contentious moral and political issues (which many education issues also touch on). From their work across 11 experiments, they find that 'despite its intuitive appeal for reducing conflict, opting not to take sides over moralised issues can harm trust, even relative to siding against an observer's viewpoint outright' (p. 2542). Staying out of the fray, they explain, is often interpreted as both deceptive and untrustworthy, and so would undermine collaboration.

It was also pointed out that by adopting a neutral role, participants were unable to access ASLs' expertise, which was a key constraint around their action plan to improve collaboration. Furthermore, while they acted as if they were neutral, ASLs were demonstrably not neutral; they did have views and opinions but chose not to disclose them. Not only were they in formal kāhui ako roles and charged with undertaking the direction of the kāhui ako principal, but they were also senior teachers within their schools and more generally subject-matter experts of the working groups they chaired. They were also required to report back on progress made towards their curricular aims and had considerable decision-making authority for the direction of working groups. Positioning themselves as neutral facilitators had the potential to hinder any progress they wished to make with the working groups as well as the working relationships they had with working group members (Schwarz, 2016).

Neutrality, we know from friendship studies, is not a strategy for strengthening relationships. In fact, people have been shown to have negative reactions towards friends who remain neutral, and negative reactions that are just as strong as those towards friends who actively oppose them (Shaw et al., 2017). And so, declaring, inviting and engaging with difference is an important strategy for building relationships and progressing joint work.

9

HUI 4 – SHOES OF OTHERS

In this chapter, we detail the intervention approach we took in Hui 4, a hui focussed on improving action plans through participants stepping into the shoes of others in a step-back consulting approach (Fig. 16).

Our final hui extended the critical aspect that Hui 3 had introduced to our intervention. We brought the two kāhui ako back together to further refine their social network improvement action plans using step-back consulting, a conversational architecture specifically designed to facilitate critical reflection on existing work (Chua & Edmonds, 2017). Step-back consulting is a protocol by which project proposals can be critiqued in an objective yet collaborative forum (Chua & Edmonds, 2017; Gillispie & Chrispeels, 2008; Jordan et al., 2019). Although its architecture is seductively simple, such structured and systematic approaches to analysing problem solving have been shown to help participants understand how they have come to conceive the problems they are solving and interrogate their preferred solutions, and therefore make possible and plausible alternative framings and solutions

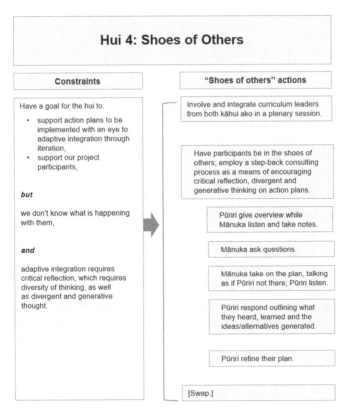

Fig. 16. Theory of Action: Hui 4 – Shoes of Others.

(Argyris, Putnam, & Smith, 1985; Chua & Edmonds, 2017; Gillispie & Chrispeels, 2008; Jordan et al., 2019; Razer, 2021).

The basic process of step-back consulting (Fig. 17.) consists of one group presenting their project plan to a second, which is unfamiliar with both the people and plan involved, in a deliberately short amount of time. The deliberately short amount of time is necessary so that the person explaining cannot get those listening to start thinking about the problem in the same way as they do – the idea is not to convert those listening to the logic underpinning the action plan, but to know enough that they can then question that logic.

The first group 'steps back' as the second group asks clarifying questions and then 'takes on' the plan, discussing as if it were their own, as if the first group was not present. Meanwhile, the first group silently observes, taking notes but neither interrupting nor responding. Once finished, the first group then responds to the second, noting what they have heard, their reactions, and what they have learned. In our hui, we then took time for both kāhui ako groups to debrief and consider their plans in light of the step-back process they had undertaken, before repeating it with the roles reversed.

We organised for the Pūriri kāhui ako to lead the session and present their action plan to the Mānuka kāhui ako. Our rationale was that, as their action plan was significantly more advanced than that of the Mānuka kāhui ako, they would provide a model of what a social network improvement action plan might look like that would spur the thinking of the Mānuka kāhui ako. They would also receive valuable feedback. As the Mānuka kāhui ako had neither progressed their action plan nor were overly familiar with the Pūriri plan and curriculum leaders, they would be giving feedback essentially as nonexpert observers (Chua & Edmonds, 2017). The view of nonexperts is useful because they inevitably 'misinterpret' or 'miscontextualise' a situation and in so doing produce new ways of viewing that reality (Chua & Edmonds, 2017). That is not to say they get it wrong, but rather that through bringing a different set of constraints, born of their own experience and knowledge, to bear on the problem, they necessarily frame it differently. Through hearing 'outsiders' discussing how they would enact their plan, the assumptions and reasoning underpinning each kāhui ako's action plan will be unfrozen.

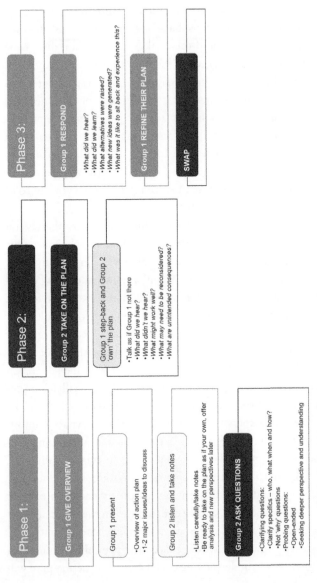

Phase 1:

Group 1 GIVE OVERVIEW

Group 1 present
- Overview of action plan
- 1-2 major issues/ideas to discuss

Group 2 listen and take notes
- Listen carefully/take notes
- Be ready to take on the plan as if your own, offer analysis and new perspectives later

Group 2 ASK QUESTIONS
- Clarifying questions:
  - Clarify specifics – who, what when and how?
  - Not why questions
- Probing questions:
  - Open-ended
  - Seeking deeper perspective and understanding

Phase 2:

Group 2 TAKE ON THE PLAN

Group 1 step-back and Group 2 'own' the plan
- Talk as if Group 1 not there
  - What did we hear?
  - What didn't we hear?
  - What might work well?
  - What may need to be reconsidered?
  - What are unintended consequences?

Phase 3:

Group 1 RESPOND
- What did we hear?
- What did we learn?
- What alternatives were raised?
- What new ideas were generated?
- What was it like to sit back and experience this?

Group 1 REFINE THEIR PLAN

SWAP

Fig. 17. Step-Back Consulting Process.

UNFREEZING

The Lewinian concept of unfreezing (Cummings, Bridgman, & Brown, 2016; Lewin, 1947) refers to people becoming cognisant of the reasoning and assumptions underpinning their actions in ways that challenge their perceptions (Friedman, 2011). Making that reasoning and the assumptions apparent allows them to consider alternative reasonings, to 'see the same situation in a new way' (Friedman, 2011, p. 250). We hoped that by listening closely to others discussing how they might enact their plan, the participants would learn more about how others, who had not been involved in designing the plan but were required to help implement it, might perceive it, and the barriers they might see to its implementation. It is important to note that in step-back consulting, people are not evaluating the plan as to its perceived effectiveness or desirability. Rather, they discuss the plan at a much more fundamental level, asking such questions as how they might go about implementing it; what might work and what might not; how the ideas in it tally with their experiences; and, from such discussion, provide alternative actions that might achieve similar results. The intention is that the people presenting the plans are offered a different perspective on how their social networks might be reconstituted. As Riordan (1995) put it, 'there has to be an unfreezing of inherited perspectives if practitioners in a group are to revise their operative assumptions and adopt new ways of thinking and acting' (p. 11). Such information is vital to ensuring the action plans are implementable and diverge from existing ways of thinking and acting.

An example of such unfreezing came when the Pūriri kāhui ako were considering what the Mānuka kāhui ako had said while discussing their plan. The Pūriri ASLs presented the idea of using Google Classrooms as a platform for across-school collaboration and sharing expertise. The Mānuka group sub-sequently took up the discussion point and noted that it was not a platform common across all of their schools. They then discussed possible solutions. The first was finding a digital platform that was agreeable to all schools. One Mānuka member then pointed out that they could simply cater to schools' existing platforms – the platform was less impor-tant than the content to be shared. When the Pūriri kāhui ako came to debrief what the Mānuka participants had said, one Pūriri kāhui ako ASL noted that they

> *hadn't considered that we don't have to use the*
> *same platform, and if there's an easier platform for*
> *our ECEs [early childhood education] to connect*
> *with, then it makes sense to follow them, so thanks*
> *for that.*

In this instance, the step-back consulting conversation prompted the Pūriri kāhui ako team to reframe their issue from needing to convert schools to using a shared platform to access knowledge and content, to thinking about how that knowledge and content could be shared across the platforms schools were using. Rather than attempting to change schools to the ways of the ASL group, they shifted to changing the way the ASL group integrated with the ways of the schools. The Pūriri ASL had found a way of working that diverged from their existing preconceptions and thinking.

DIVERGENT AND GENERATIVE THINKING

Divergent thinking refers to the generation of different solu-tions to a problem through the comparison and combination of information in new ways (Acar & Runco, 2019; Runco, 2019). The architecture of step-back consulting itself provides a protocol whereby new information is generated by the party 'taking on' the plan, which can then be compared and recombined with the information of the existing action plan to create new ideas that would not have been possible without the input of the nonexpert observer. The unfrozen existing framing of the problem is able to be compared with that of the 'misinterpreted' framing of the nonexpert, sparking the creative recombination of ideas. By exposing our participants to divergent thought, we hoped to spur generative thinking.

Generative thinking, or the construction of a novel way of conceiving a familiar concept (Schön, 1993; Ward, Smith, & Vaid, 1997; Ward & Sifonis, 1997), results in new perceptions, explanations and inventions. Any new idea created will share similarities with those already described, reflecting a mix of old and new properties (Ward & Sifonis, 1997). For the Pūriri kāhui ako, we were not expecting wholesale changes to an already well-developed action plan, but rather a refinement of their ideas stemming from a reexamination of them in light of their discussion by the Mānuka kāhui ako participants. The Pūriri participants would in turn bring their experience in developing an action plan to improve a social network to the very basic ideas and problematic patterns of the Mānuka kāhui ako, allowing them firstly to conceive that solutions to such problems were possible, and secondly to provide them with the sort of cognitive processes required to invent and refine such ideas.

In fact, there were signs that kāhui ako members did experience divergent thinking leading to generative thinking as a result of the step-back consulting process. For example, during their presentation of their action plan, the Pūriri kāhui ako ASLs mentioned their working groups, describing how they had been arranged to take place during the in-school time. When considering the Pūriri action plan, the working groups stood out to the Mānuka participants because to take

place during school time, they had to be funded. One of the
Mānuka ASLs noted they were

> *not aware we've been able to do, that so that's*
> *something to consider ... it would be interesting to*
> *find out where they get that funding from, how they*
> *do it.*

When subsequently working on their own action plan, the
previous discussion led the Mānuka kāhui ako to recall their
own attempts at such work, using what they called 'PLCs'
(professional learning communities). One of the Mānuka
teachers stated that their schools 'thrived' on face-to-face contact, which led to a further discussion about how, and why,
those PLCs had 'petered out'. It was decided that the main
problem was a logistical one: the PLCs had operated before
and after school, which meant teachers often had trouble getting to them and attendance had dwindled to maybe four or
five people. As a result of that and COVID-19 precautions,
most of their work had moved online. It was also noted, however, that the change to online work had 'changed the type
of work' they were doing. The result of this discussion was a
reframing by the Mānuka participants that their main problem was a lack of balance between online and face-to-face
interactions. Face-to-face interactions would create the relationships necessary to build engagement with online work.
Therefore, they redesigned their action plan to address that
imbalance.

Their redesigned action plan constituted three interlinked
components with which they could ensure a better balance
between online and face-to-face interaction. Firstly, they
would upgrade their kāhui ako website and refocus the content on it so that it was a better platform for sharing knowledge and expertise across schools. Secondly, they would
reinstitute their PLCs. The low, previous attendance of the

PLCs was reframed as a positive. As one of the Mānuka ASLs noted, 'you might only have five people, but they might go to three different schools and cascade information'. PLCs and other meetings could be recorded and embedded in the kāhui ako website, which would serve as a hub for all kāhui ako-related content. Finally, they would look to address what they termed the 'accessibility' challenges to attending PLC meetings, which meant finding out what was preventing people from attending them: were they logistical issues such as a lack of time or reluctance because the purpose of the PLC meetings was unclear?

After being given such a well-reasoned action plan, with clear links between the perceived problem causes and proposed actions, the Pūriri kāhui ako were able to take it on by focussing very closely on the proposed actions and the reasoning underpinning them. For example, one Pūriri ASL mentioned that there had been considerable resistance by some teachers within their kāhui ako to recording meetings and that doing so often changed the nature of discussions within meetings. This comment on recording meetings spurred one of the Mānuka kāhui ako curriculum leaders to note that their school prohibited recordings of female teachers and students, meaning a key new constraint was unearthed that the Mānuka kāhui ako would have to consider when implementing their action plan. Another Pūriri ASL noted that one possible way of mitigating the poor attendance of PLCs, which they described as 'exciting', might be to come to an agreement on a smaller optimum size for them and then focus on who they could specifically invite to attend. A further Pūriri curriculum leader then noted that the Mānuka kāhui ako could approach the kāhui ako leadership and try to utilise kāhui ako funding so that their PLCs could take place during the school day.

As a result of both the ASL planning day and feedback from the Mānuka kāhui and their kāhui ako peers during the step-back-consulting hui, the Pūriri kāhui ako ASLs refined their action plan so that it included several new action strategies. The first was to develop a means to connect in a virtual and asynchronous way by using a platform such as Google Classroom to provide a channel for more staff to contact with each other to build collaborative relationships. Within Google Classroom, they would create a folder containing short videos showing staff expertise that they would post once a week. They would also use Google Classroom to share personal inquiries and explicitly invite others to join. A second set of action strategies was to do with their current working groups. They decided to continue with them, but would promote and communicate a simple and easy-to-understand summary of kāhui ako objectives and key contact people. Such communication would more clearly clarify the purpose of each workgroup and enable staff to identify and access experience and expertise within the kāhui ako. In addition, along with the ASL leading the working group, they decided to have another attend as an observer who would note any points of agreement, collaboration, shared concerns, or priorities that arose. From the working group sessions, the two ASLs would then create action plans and post them back to attendees. A final action strategy was to increase the frequency of formal and informal connections across the kāhui ako by having people from different schools speak about the kāhui ako across-school work to school staff every two weeks at staff and school meetings.

The step-back-consulting day ended with a debriefing of the process the participants had undertaken. The important point of ensuring a tight link between causes and solutions in action plans was reinforced. As a final exercise, participants were asked to move from the abstract to the specific in terms of actions they would take by completing, on a Post-It note, the sentence, 'As a result of today, I will/am going to …' Some typical responses included the following:

- I am going to attend the PLCs.

- I am going to reconnect with WSLs [within-school leaders] across my kāhui ako.

- I am going to address current challenges and barriers with principals.

- I will initiate more collaboration with neighbouring schools.

- I am going to clearly communicate the purposes of our workshops.

- I am going to give 30-minutes time in staff meetings for updates.

- I am going to continue to support releasing people.

- I am going to write a communications plan and explore other kāhui ako structures.

PART 3

INTERVENTION IMPACT AND LOOKING FORWARD

At its heart, the Better Together project had the important and ambitious goal of strengthening the relational infrastructures within each kāhui ako and all aspects of our intervention work focussed on human relations and SNA provided a theoretical frame and a methodological toolbox through which we examined the social side of the work in these educational networks. The social relations in professional learning networks are critical in providing conditions conducive to the realisation of the aspirations set out in curriculum reform (at a system level) and curriculum change (including those at more local levels).

In the following chapters, we present our findings from that analysis. In Chapter 10, we present the big picture (a summary of shifts in the right direction between time 1 and time 2) and follow by sharing more particular shifts and findings relating to network intentionality. We finish, in Chapter 11, by offering a framework of considerations for social network interventions for curriculum improving, drawing on insights from our work here.

10

SHIFTS IN THE RELATIONAL SPACE

NETWORK IMPROVEMENT – THE BIG PICTURE

The network maps in Figs. 18 and 19 show us the big picture. They visualise the interactions among and between people within each kāhui ako. Recall that we can consider network relations – called 'ties' in network terminology – from the point of view of quantity (i.e. the frequency of interaction) and quality (i.e. the strength of the tie). In doing so, we were able to examine the networks within different temporal frames. For instance, these network maps show the patterns of interaction at the termly level – that is, ties with a reported frequency of at least once per term. What they show us is that, overall, there was growth in collaboration ties in both kāhui ako over time. In other words, the collaborative work within each kāhui ako was cultivating relational space that increased the levels of interaction among participants; the networks were moving in the right direction.

What does it mean to be moving in the right direction? Given the policy context in New Zealand and the wider

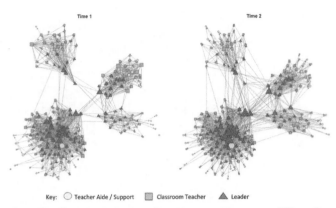

Fig. 18.   Termly Collaboration Maps at Time 1 and Time 2 in the Pūriri Kāhui Ako.

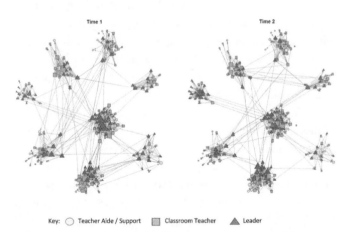

Fig. 19.   Termly Collaboration Maps at Time 1 and Time 2 in the Mānuka Kāhui Ako.

world and the focus on sharing knowledge and resources through collaborative work within a kāhui ako, moving in the right direction meant building a relational infrastructure that supported knowledge and resource exchange. The greater the number of interactions that comprised a social network, the more easily resources could be accessed and exchanged by its members. The more that patterns of relationship spread across the entirety of the group, the less influence and control some individuals could wield over the mobilisation of resources within the group. The more often people made new connections, the greater their access to new forms of knowledge and resources. Moving in the right direction means that more educators were gaining access to diverse resources from a variety of sources that assisted in the effective development and implementation of curriculum that supports learners with diverse learning needs.

In order to examine the shifts in relational space, we used network measures to characterise precisely the relational patterns; network maps on their own were insufficient. As such, our team selected a number of commonly used measures that describe the patterns of interaction across the whole network. Fig. 20 provides a summary of the movement of network measures in each kāhui ako. White cells indicate network measures that show areas where the relational patterns require further work whereas the shaded cells indicate areas of growth. The overall pattern was one of shifts in the right direction; we saw improvement in the vast majority of whole network measures we looked at, across all of the relational tie types we examined.

In the next section, we take these network measures and dive into the particulars. We look at the growth in ties overall, how many people remained disconnected, who were the most frequently sought-out people in the network and so on. Doing so allows us to bring the bigger picture into greater focus, identifying areas of strength and weakness in the networks and providing valuable insights to guide future action.

	Puriri								Manuka								
	Advice			Collaboration			Materials	Close Relation-ship	Advice			Collaboration			Go to	Materials	Close Relation-ship
	Yearly	Termly	Monthly	Yearly	Termly	Monthly			Yearly	Termly	Monthly	Yearly	Termly	Monthly			
# of ties	10%	9%	1%	7%	13%	12%	6%	28%	27%	12%	5%	13%	8%	-1%	7%	21%	0%
# of isolates	0%	0%	100%	0%	-100%	-88%	-31%	-50%	0%	100%	0%	-25%	25%	57%	50%	-75%	150%
Avg Degree	10%	9%	1%	7%	13%	12%	6%	28%	27%	12%	5%	13%	8%	-1%	7%	21%	0%
Density	11%	10%	0%	6%	16%	14%	8%	28%	25%	11%	7%	12%	8%	0%	5%	22%	8%
Fragmentation	-14%	-21%	-18%	12%	-3%	-23%	-16%	-17%	-3%	3%	6%	-19%	-3%	23%	-18%	3%	-3%
Reciprocity	5%	7%	6%	8%	1%	0%	-1%	7%	12%	19%	31%	4%	4%	5%	29%	17%	4%
Deg centralisation	-43%	19%	31%	-47%	15%	13%	13%	166%	53%	-30%	-24%	-41%	-44%	-51%	-50%	-24%	-7%
Out-centralisation	-47%	30%	41%	-45%	17%	13%	13%	213%	46%	-31%	-26%	-38%	-41%	-49%	-49%	-29%	-6%
In-centralisation	3%	1%	7%	6%	-4%	-19%	-7%	5%	-22%	-21%	13%	40%	54%	47%	23%	-14%	-13%
Avg distance	-5%	-10%	-7%	-10%	-20%	-10%	-20%	-17%	-22%	-8%	-13%	-1%	1%	-21%	-3%	-14%	7%
Prop within 3	9%	28%	21%	17%	51%	45%	49%	54%	51%	10%	17%	13%	2%	2%	25%	32%	-6%
SD distance	-9%	-21%	-12%	-19%	-37%	-21%	-35%	-18%	-37%	-17%	-12%	-2%	1%	-23%	-1%	-4%	12%
Diameter	0%	-25%	13%	-14%	-40%	-20%	-17%	-11%	-29%	-17%	23%	10%	0%	-33%	0%	-15%	14%

Fig. 20. Schematic Representing Shifts in the Right Direction in Whole Network Measures.

NETWORK IMPROVEMENT – SOME PARTICULARS

To learn about the social dynamics of relational spaces, we need tools to help bring 'the space between' into focus. SNA does just that. It enables us to consider social networks from multiple vantage points. First, we considered the network as a whole using measures of *network cohesion*. Cohesion describes the degree of connectivity in a network. It encompasses numerous measures, including density, centralisation, fragmentation and reciprocity – all of which help us understand the extent to which actors are able to access the resources that are available within the network. We also considered the network from the perspective of each individual actor in the network using measures of *centrality*. Centrality measures focus on the prominence and prestige of individual actors, identifying those individuals who hold power and influence within the social network.

In the following sections, we examine cohesion and centrality with selected SNA measures, providing an explanation of what the data means and why it matters. Accordingly, this is a highly technical chapter. While we endeavour to explain these statistics in nontechnical terms, it is important to dive into these particulars to show the depth of this work and demonstrate how the social infrastructure across these networks changed over time.

More Ties Overall With Fewer Isolates

The starting point with SNA is to consider the total number of ties present in a network. Most often, the goal in social network contexts is to increase connectivity; indeed, this was the goal of the Better Together project. Our research shows that, between T1 and T2 (an approximately 18-month period), the number of relational ties increased in both kāhui ako across virtually all of the relational dimensions we queried. This means that all educators participating in the kāhui ako had more opportunities to access the different resources (i.e. advice, collaboration, curriculum expertise, materials, encourage-ment, energy and close professional relationships) available to them in this network. With the exception of monthly collabo-ration and close professional relationship ties in Mānuka, the majority of relational dimensions in both Mānuka and Pūriri kāhui ako experienced growth ranging from 1% to 29%.

Along with this growth in ties, we also witnessed a concomi-tant *reduction* in the number of people who were *not* involved in this network (i.e. isolates) in some relational dimensions; meaning there were fewer isolated people in the network. The Pūriri kāhui ako, in particular, experienced a tremendous decline in the number of isolates in their collaboration net-work. All respondents reported at least one termly collabo-ration tie and there was a single isolate in the collaboration network at the monthly interval (a reduction of nearly 90%). In the Mānuka kāhui ako, there was a 75% reduction in the number of isolates in the materials network with all but three individuals reporting materials exchange with their colleagues in their network community. Overall, these network statistics demonstrate that the social networks within each kāhui ako grew in total number of ties present and that more people became connected to others in multiple relational dimensions. As a result, the potential for resource exchange within these networks increased by providing the network members more numerous opportunities to connect with their colleagues.

Greater Proportion of All Possible Ties Being Activated

With what proportion of the potential connections in this network are people actually connecting? To what extent are people interconnected? Network *density* is an important network measure as it answers these questions; it describes the number of ties that exist in a network as a proportion of the total number of ties possible in a network. In a network with a density score of 100% (D = 1.0), each actor is connected to each and every other actor in the network. In the Mānuka kāhui ako, for example, the yearly advice network had a density of 4.4% at Time 1. This means that for every 100 *possible ties*, about four ties were present. At Time 2, the network density had increased to 5.5%, an increase of 25%. It is a human tendency to want to draw a line between what constitutes a 'good' or 'bad' network density score; human brains love simplicity. However, these distinctions are not so simple given that network density is a measure that is extremely sensitive to network size (i.e. the total number of actors in a network). The smaller the network, the easier it is to achieve high levels of network density. The larger the network, the more difficult it is for everyone to be connected to everyone else. Hence, it is best to observe density in relation to itself within a network over time.

In the Pūriri kāhui ako, growth in network density ranged from 0% in the proportion of monthly advice ties to 29% in close professional relationships, indicating strong growth in relational social capital. Similarly, in the Mānuka kāhui ako, growth in network density ranged from 0% (monthly collaboration ties) to 25% (yearly advice ties). An increase in a network density score is an indicator of the strengthening of a network because it signifies an improvement in access to resources – the denser the network, the greater the access potential. In this way, it is similar to the total measure of ties; density increases as the number of ties increases in a network, thereby providing a greater number of pathways within the network through which people can connect with each other.

Lower Percentage of People Who Cannot Reach Each Other

Fragmentation is another network cohesion measure that provides important information about people's access to resources. It responds to the question, how difficult is it for people to access the resources in the network? This measure reports the percentage of pairs of nodes that cannot reach each other. That is, given the observed patterns of interactions in a network, these pairs are people who are unable to connect with each other either directly or indirectly. It is the inverse of connectedness. When a fragmentation score equals 100%, it means that it is an entirely disconnected network; no one can access the resources of anyone else.

Both the Mānuka and Pūriri kāhui ako demonstrated reductions in network fragmentation from Time 1 to Time 2. The Pūriri community saw reductions in fragmentation across all but one relational dimension (yearly collaboration ties being the exception) with reductions ranging from 3% to 23%. The greatest increase in access occurred in the termly advice ties (–21%) and monthly collaboration ties (–23%). Similarly, the Mānuka community saw reductions in more than half of the relational dimensions, ranging from 3% to 18%. While some networks, unfortunately, witnessed a decrease in access (e.g. fragmentation in monthly collaboration ties increased by 23%), other networks increased access (e.g. fragmentation in the go-to network decreased by 18%). Thus, while some relational dimensions provide better opportunities for resource access than others, a takeaway from this study is that, overall (and particularly in the Pūriri kāhui ako), networks strengthened as a greater proportion of people within the network gained access to the social capital available to them within it (i.e. resources exchanged through social relationships).

More People Are Developing Mutual Relationships
with Colleagues

Resources can flow in two ways. Claire can give advice to Joelle, and Joelle can give advice to Claire. Darren can provide materials to Alan, and Alan can provide materials to Darren. *Reciprocity* is a network measure that provides insight into the proportions of relational pairs (e.g. Claire–Joelle, Darren–Alan) in a network which are providing resources to each other. It answers the question, are relationships among the actors in a network mutual? Do members of each pair receive resources from each other or is resource flow unidirectional? From a social network point of view, reciprocal ties are more durable; they are considered stronger ties than those where resources flow in one direction only. A stronger relationship exists, for example, when Claire and Joelle are *both seeking and providing resources* to each other. When networks experience an increase in the proportion of reciprocal ties, we consider the network to be strengthening.

The Pūriri kāhui ako experienced growth in reciprocal ties across the majority of its relational dimensions. Growth patterns ranged from 1% to 8% with some dimensions experiencing no change (monthly collaboration ties) or a reduction in reciprocity (e.g. reciprocated close professional relationship ties decreased by 7%). The Mānuka kāhui ako experienced much larger gains in reciprocity across all relational dimensions, ranging from 4% to 31%. Monthly advice ties increased in reciprocity by 31% and the go-to network also increased by 29%. Overall, despite a few exceptions, both of these kāhui ako demonstrated shifts in relational patterns that indicate the strengthening of the networks from the perspective of mutual ties.

Ease of Access to Resources Is Improving

We can use multiple social network measures to determine the ease of access people have to each other in their social networks. *Average distance*, for example, determines the average number of 'steps' it would take to access everyone in the network given the relational pattern of the network. The higher the number of steps, the more difficult it is to access resources (i.e. the more people who would have to serve as resource connectors). Relatedly, *proportion within 3* reports the proportion of actors within a network that an individual can access within three steps; the higher the proportion, the more compact the network is, thereby providing greater access to resources. *Standard deviation (SD) distance* measures how much variation there is in terms of individuals' access to resources in the network. If an individual has an average distance of 2.1 and the SD is 0.8, for example, then 68% of the people in the network can access a resource on average between 1.3 and 2.9 steps (i.e. 2.1 +/– 0.8, or the mean score +/– one SD). Considered together, these measures provide a robust characterisation of the increasing ease of access members have to potential resources in the network.

In the Pūriri kāhui ako, the monthly collaboration network had tremendous growth in access. The average distance decreased by 10% and the proportion within 3 increased by 45%. Variation, as measured by SD distance, decreased by 21%. This pattern demonstrates a strengthening of access overall, a pattern that is repeated in the monthly advice, materials and close professional relationships network dimensions. Similarly, many relational dimensions in the Mānuka kāhui ako also followed this pattern of strengthening with a decrease in average distance and SD, and an increase in the proportion of network actors accessible within three steps.

The materials network, for example, showed strong signs of positive relational shifts with a 14% reduction in average distance, a 4% decrease in SD, and a substantial increase of 32% in the proportion of actors reachable within three steps. Collectively, across all relational dimensions in both kāhui ako, these measures also demonstrate that the networks strengthened over time.

Increase in the Number of People to Whom One Is Connected

Thus far, our measures have focussed on the network level, using tools to describe relational patterns at the aggregate level. But we can ask questions that focus on the individual level as well; for example, how many others do people connect with on average? Degree centrality measures the number of connections an actor has in a network. Average degree provides network analysts with an idea of the average number of ties an individual maintains within a network. In practical terms, gains in average degree relate to increases in potential access to a wider variety of resources given the increased opportunities afforded by the growth in direct and indirect social ties.

In these two communities, across nearly all relational dimensions, there was growth in average degree scores, ranging from 0% to 27%. In the Pūriri kāhui ako, for example, termly collaboration ties increased by 15% and monthly collaboration ties increased by 12%. Similarly, in the Mānuka kāhui ako, termly advice ties increased by 12%. While gains in degree may seem small, it is important to take into account that when a person in a network gains one additional direct tie, they also gain indirect ties with that person's social network.

Some People Are More Central Than Others

Across these social networks, there are two classes of actors: those who are seeking resources and those who are providing resources. While the networks became denser and people became more connected through increased interactions (in terms of seeking and providing), a category of network measures called *degree centralisation* (CD) shows that some people are more active than others. The higher the CD score is to 100% (or 1.0), the more the activity within that network focusses on an identifiable subset of people. When we have data that indicate who are the resources seekers and who are the resource providers in a network – as we do here – we can further break the concept down into two subcategories: *out-centralisation*, which emphasises resource seekers, and *in-centralisation*, which focusses on resource providers.

These measures are highly variable. In many cases, centralisation was low, with scores less than 30%. In the Pūriri kāhui ako, centralisation was most challenging at the level of yearly advice and collaboration ties. At Time 1, for example, the yearly advice-tie pattern indicated that 88.9% of the ties present in the network focussed on a particular subset of people. Fortunately, the centralisation score for termly advice ties was reduced by 48% at Time 2, with the centralisation score falling to 46.5%. As such, the community had greater access to resources without relationships requiring mediation from highly central individuals.

The Mānuka kāhui ako illustrates a near universal decline in degree centralisation across all relational dimensions. This pattern persists when one considers the directionality of resource flow. The centralisation of resource-seeking behaviour (i.e. out-centralisation) also reduced across almost all relational dimensions meaning that more people were actively seeking out support in the kāhui ako. Conversely, in-degree centralisation scores increased across the majority of relational dimensions; however, it is notable that these scores were very low to begin with, most often with resource provision ties focussed on less than 10% of educators.

There are important practical implications for such structural features given that highly centralised networks are known to constrain resource mobilisation – that is, it is much more difficult for resources to flow among and between actors within a network (Wasserman, 1994). Furthermore, individuals who occupy central positions within a network can also hold a position of power, potentially gatekeeping the types of resources that are flowing within a network (Prell, 2012). This centralisation of power over resource mobilisation can act as a significant constraint on an individual's ability to access the resources required to ensure effective learning environments for students.

CHANGE IN NETWORK-LEADER BEHAVIOUR: INCREASED NETWORK INTENTIONALITY

While network maps and measures provide valuable information to describe social patterns within a group such as a kāhui ako, they also provide valuable information that can inform future action. That was the goal (and the outcome) of the Better Together project. To complement our understanding of relational patterns in the two, we also asked questions about network intentionality (see Chapter 5). Our analysis yielded important insights into how educators view the importance of social networks. Overall, educators in the Pūriri and Mānuka kāhui ako noted the importance of having the right set of relationships for improving their instructional quality. Despite these beliefs, however, they report less intentionality about their actions in cultivating relationships with others. Educators who intentionally seek out relationships with colleagues are significantly more likely to have higher out-degree (i.e. report a higher number of resource-seeking ties) for curriculum-related resources or materials. In general, when educators actively engage in their networks and consider themselves to be a point of connection within the network, they play key roles in connection to other people who may otherwise be disconnected in the network. The desire to connect with or help others has a significant positive effect on in-degree centrality (i.e. the number of times that person is identified as a source of information). Educators who possess beliefs about quality personal networks and the importance of connecting with others are also more likely to be sought out for advice, collaboration and materials (i.e. higher in-degree centrality). Within this context, across both kāhui ako, people are more likely to form ties with others who work in the same school or who have the same role within the system.

Table 10 provides a comparative overview of network intentionality between kāhui ako and senior school leaders and school middle leaders and teachers. Senior leaders (at the school and kāhui ako level) show higher levels of network intentionality than those in other 'lower' positions (in terms of the formal organisational hierarchy) – particularly in terms of their beliefs about networks and connecting with others. Some roles naturally provide increased opportunities for networking (e.g. senior leadership) whereas the day-to-day of other roles (e.g. teaching) provides fewer opportunities to connect with others, especially with those who may not work within the 'functional zone' of the classroom teacher (Spillane, Shirrell, & Sweet, 2017). The work for leaders in this context is to focus attention on increasing the potential for networking for the folks in their schools – for those whose typical workday is confined to a particular place in the school

Table 10. Network Intentionality by Role (Time 2)

Network Intentionality	Kāhui ako and School Senior Leaders			School Middle Leaders and Teachers					
	N	Mean	SD	N	Mean	SD	Diff.	Sig.	Cohen's d
Seek	67	4.63	0.67	324	4.42	0.92	−0.21	0.03	0.24
Beliefs	67	5.17	0.64	324	5.06	0.68	−0.11	0.22	0.16
Assess	67	4.15	1.05	324	3.92	1.02	−0.23	0.10	0.22
Connect	67	4.70	0.79	324	4.36	0.79	−0.34	0.00	0.43

Note. Items were rated on a 6-point scale where 1 = strongly disagree and 6 = strongly agree.

(i.e. a classroom), which naturally constrains their ability to connect with others in terms of time and proximity.

To some extent, the structure of a person's social network is out of their control as they cannot dictate who holds relationships with whom (i.e. the relational space that surrounds them). However, each person has the ability to influence the structure of their network with the set of direct connections that they choose to cultivate and nurture. The network intentionality helps researchers *and participants* understand the extent to which their beliefs are congruent with their actions. Is a belief that having the right set of relationships to achieve a goal is sufficient in motivating action to develop those relationships? We suggest that it is not. A favourable disposition towards connecting with others is not beneficial if one is not actually carrying through with the requisite relational work to build and maintain those relationships. Measuring network intentionality alongside network mapping can be a provocative exercise when these learnings are shared with the people involved in a network.

As part of the intervention, participants came together in a hui where results from the network surveys were shared and members of each kāhui ako were led through a variety of exercises to help understand and cultivate relational spaces that support educators' curricular work in schools. As part of a feedback process, hui evaluation forms were distributed in which participants were asked to rate the extent to which participation in the hui helped them think about the social networks in their school and broader learning community. Table 11 provides an overview of the findings from the questions that centred on network intentionality. The questionnaire items are ordered from highest ranked to lowest ranked when combined into one group across the two kāhui ako.

Table 11. **Impact of Intervention on Network Intentionality.**

The hui has...	Combined (Pūriri + Mānuka)		
	Mean	Min	Max
increased my intention to make use of existing relationships across our community of learning (CoL).	5.17	4	6
increased my awareness of the patterns of relationships in our CoL.	5.06	4	6
increased my intention to create new relationships across our CoL.	5.06	4	6
increased my intention to make use of existing relationships in our school.	5.00	1	6
highlighted some untapped relationship potential in our CoL.	4.97	3	6
motivated me to do something about the patterns of relationships in our CoL.	4.94	4	6
confirmed some of the things I thought about the patterns of relationships in our CoL.	4.94	4	6
helped me to connect with a new colleague.	4.94	3	6
increased my intention to create new relationships in our school.	4.80	2	6
deepened my understanding of social network analysis and its link to curriculum problem solving.	4.80	3	6
revealed some surprises in the patterns of relationships in our CoL.	4.66	2	6
helped prepare us to craft an action plan.	4.60	3	6

Note. Items were rated on a 6-point scale where 1 = strongly disagree and 6 = strongly agree.

As demonstrated in the Better Together project, network data (e.g. maps, network intentionality scale, feedback) helped individuals assess their own professional networks, both within their school and across their kāhui ako. This type of information can prove important to assist educators' action plans as they begin to seek out relationships with colleagues to access the resources they need.

MOVING IN THE RIGHT DIRECTION: KĀHUI AKO NETWORKS ARE STRENGTHENING

Daily life in schools and school systems has long been described as a complex system (see Lortie, 1975, for example). Research in education often focusses on the various aspects of these systems – policy, curriculum, instruction, assessment practices and so on – but it rarely focusses on the social infrastructure that supports this work (Daly, 2010; Quintero, 2017). In the Better Together project, our focus included *explicit attention* to network development in a quest to build relational infrastructures within multiple kāhui ako that facilitate greater access to the resources necessary to build effective schools and school systems. The network data presented for both the Pūriri and Mānuka kāhui ako in this chapter demonstrate that relationships within both these communities of learning are strengthening. There was a growth in activity as more people connected with others, yielding denser networks that provide educators with greater opportunities to access the various resources within the system. While the depth of growth varied across the different relational dimensions, the general pattern across the networks demonstrates that relational patterns are strengthening; people are more easily able to access each other as the network strengthens over time. This is good news. It means that curriculum change occurring in meaningful ways becomes more likely. That said, measures such as centralisation, which show that network activity can sometimes cluster around particular groups of people, provide useful information to inform future work. In this context, networks strengthen as more educators become involved in supporting each other's practice through resource exchange.

So what does this mean for others and for the design of social network interventions going forward? We turn our attention to that next.

11

LOOKING BACK TO MOVE FORWARD

Curriculum reform is critical for ensuring that educators' efforts serve diverse learners well and reflect the vision and priorities of their communities and society. Curriculum is also an essential lever for advancing equity and excellence in education. The success of curriculum reform efforts is highly dependent on a combination of human *and* social capital. Initiatives focussed on human capital, including the knowledge, skills and capabilities of educators' have a long history in education. For example, we develop resources to help teachers understand what curriculum changes are, we construct tools to exemplify new possibilities for enacting the curriculum, and we offer professional learning opportunities to help teachers to make changes to their practice in line with new curricula. More recently, in some jurisdictions, recognition of the social side of curriculum reform is gaining momentum. Policy makers, practitioners, leaders and other stakeholders in educational contexts, keen to disrupt typical patterns of failed or at least not fully successful curriculum reform, are paying attention to the relational conditions that are essential for curriculum reform aspirations being realised.

Few would argue that deep, purposeful and sustained collaboration amongst educators in schools is not important. In most educational systems, there are policy directives and professional learning initiatives that reflect a recognition of that importance. However, despite the rhetoric about collaboration, and the good intentions of educators, more individualistic approaches and surface-level collaboration often persist.

Our work sought to help educators to recognise the power of the social capital residing in their social systems; to gain insights into how and where the resources of their own network were being realised; and to begin solving problematic patterns they noticed. The relational space we focussed on cannot be taken for granted. Unfortunately, the relational space is unlikely to improve just over the course of time, or just through the goodwill of people involved. Improving the social relations of educational networks, in ways that will build trust and strengthen the conditions in which they do their work, demands explicit attention and effort; it calls for intervention.

The Better Together intervention did support positive change in the relational space of the kāhui ako we worked with. The theory of action approach we took to thinking about and reflecting on our project design, enabled important insights that we hope will inspire similar, but not identical, efforts by others. Having shared specifics of the approach we took in earlier chapters, we turn here to what we learnt in a more general sense. How might policy makers, researchers and practitioners go about such interventions, and what ought they consider? Based on insights from our experience in our project, we propose a set of key considerations for designing social network interventions for curriculum realisation.

The considerations about social network interventions are themselves a network of ideas that intersect and interact (Fig. 21). They do not provide answers about what to do and how.

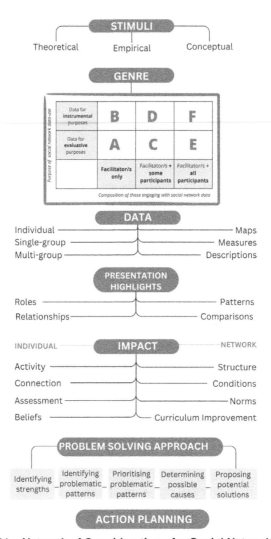

Fig. 21.   Network of Considerations for Social Network Interventions.

Rather, they are intended to provoke questions to support the design and development of others' interventions with similar goals.

Stimuli The Better Together team learnt the importance of providing participants with stimuli that ground and inspire their work, stimuli that are memorable so that the ideas in them impact leaders' immediate responses, and responses they make for the duration of their career. Those stimuli include not only theoretical ideas but also conceptual and empirical insights that inform the more practical approaches curriculum leaders can take.

Data and its presentation. The importance of generating, and sharing with leaders, robust data including data from and about their own contexts, was particularly apparent. In our case, that data came from a range of social network analyses and became a key tool for leaders to share their understanding and to engage with the data. A related and important consideration for such interventions is how to present such network data. We learnt that careful thinking about the roles and relationships to illuminate is essential to ensure that data speaks to the concerns of practitioners. Furthermore, we learnt the power of comparisons of different types to deepen understanding and provoke action. Similarly, we learnt the importance of presenting data that shows patterns of relevance to curriculum leaders and that connect with their areas of responsibility and expertise.

Genres of data use. Our learning extended to making distinctions between different genres of data use in social network interventions. The Type F genre that characterised our intervention (facilitator/s and all network members engaging with network data for improvement purposes) is just one of six we proposed (see Fig. 4); the genre that others use will depend on the particular context in which the intervention takes place, the resources available, and the goals of the project. We would urge others doing similar work to consider approaching data use in ways that serve the practical needs of the people in the networks represented by the data, and that ensure the widest engagement with the data that is possible.

Problem solving. Our learning confirmed that a problem-solving approach such as the one we used, is a productive approach to take–the solutions to the important problematic patterns determined by the two kāhui ako we worked with did not reside in us. Our role was to facilitate networks to identify their own most important patterns to address and to surface their own perspectives on how they could be logically and creatively addressed. While considering those patterns, their causes and solutions are critical to intervention efforts in this space, the specific approaches that could be used to do so are limitless.

Impact. We learnt too that the impacts of a social network intervention such as ours can be wide and varied, and so intervention designers need to be discerning in the network impacts they explore. Both individual impacts (such as impacts on network intentionality) and wider network impacts need consideration. Wider impacts include the relational conditions of the network, the norms that are at play and the extent to which curricular aspirations are realised.

At the heart of the intervention work we have shared is a view of curriculum leaders that extends beyond their role as experts in curriculum design, curriculum teaching and learning and curriculum enactment. This view takes a broader vision of leadership than is often the case; it asks curriculum leaders to attend not only to technical approaches that might support curriculum to be realised (formal structures, processes and accountabilities) but also primarily to the relational approaches that underpin all other efforts. With this in mind, curriculum leaders might ask these kinds of questions: how are we collectively maximising the interconnections amongst those within and beyond our network?; how easy is it for our people to reach the resources of others?; are we working in ways that foster reciprocity in the ties between people?; are we thinking about and actively working to connect with those who might be marginalised in our networks? And what are the problematic patterns in terms of relationships in our network, and what causes of those patterns should be reflected in the solutions we try?

It is in the relational space that trust lies and through which information, ideas and other resources critical to curriculum realisation flow. It is a space that is often invisible, but always influential, and so is an important space for curriculum leaders to focus their influence. The relational dimension of curriculum realisation efforts is also, therefore, an important focus of interventions, professional learning and research and development initiatives involving curriculum leaders. Curriculum will be better for children and young people, when the educators around them are supported to become better together.

REFERENCES

Acar, S., & Runco, M. A. (2019). Divergent thinking: New methods, recent research, and extended theory. *Psychology of Aesthetics, Creativity, and the Arts*, *13*(2), 153–158. doi:10.1037/aca0000231

Adams, A. M., Nababan, H. Y., & Hanifi, S. M. A. (2015). Building social networks for maternal and newborn health in poor urban settlements: A cross-sectional study in Bangladesh. *PLoS One*, *10*(4), e0123817.

Aitken, G. (2005). *Social studies curriculum design: Learning from the past*. Unpublished doctoral thesis, The University of Auckland.

Apple, M. W. (2015). Understanding and interrupting hegemonic projects in education: Learning from Stuart Hall. *Discourse*, *36*(2), 171. Education Database.

Argyris, C. (1976). Single-loop and double-loop models in research on decision making. *Administrative Science Quarterly*, *21*(3), 363–375. doi:10.2307/2391848

Argyris, C. (1993). *Knowledge for action: A guide to overcoming barriers to organizational change*. Jossey-Bass.

Argyris, C. (1996). Actionable knowledge: Design causality in the service of consequential theory. *The Journal of Applied Behavioral Science*, *32*(4), 390–406.

Argyris, C. (2008). *Teaching smart people how to learn: Vol. Harvard business review classics series.* Harvard Business Press.

Argyris, C., Putnam, R., & Smith, D. (1985). *Action science.* Jossey-Bass.

Argyris, C., & Schön, D. A. (1974). *Theory in practice: Increasing professional effectiveness.* Jossey-Bass.

Argyris, C., & Schön, D. (1996). *Organizational learning II: Theory, method and practice.* Addison-Wesley Publishing.

Ashmos, D. P., & Nathan, M. L. (2002). Team sense-making: A mental model for navigating uncharted territories. *Journal of Managerial Issues, 14*(2), 198–217.

Ausubel, D. P. (1962). Learning by discovery: Rationale and "mystique": Is it a feasible method? *The Education Digest, 27*(7).

Baker-Doyle, K. J., & Yoon, S. A. (2010). Making expertise transparent: Using technology to strengthen social networks in teacher professional development. In A. J. Daly (Ed.), *Social network theory and educational change* (pp. 111–126). Harvard Education Press.

Baker-Doyle, K. J., & Yoon, S. A. (2020). The social side of teacher education: Implications of social network research for the design of professional development. *International Journal of Educational Research, 101*, 101563.

Ballerini, M., Cabibbo, N., Candelier, R., Cavagna, A., Cisbani, E., Giardina, I., … Zdravkovic, V. (2008). Empirical investigation of starling flocks: A benchmark study in collective animal behaviour. *Animal Behaviour, 76*(1), 201–215. doi:10.1016/j.anbehav.2008.02.004

Bastian, L. A., Fish, L. J., Peterson, B. L., Biddle, A. K., Garst, J., Lyna, P., ... McBride, C. M. (2013). Assessment of the impact of adjunctive proactive telephone counseling to promote smoking cessation among lung cancer patients' social networks. *American Journal of Health Promotion: AJHP, 27*(3), 181–190. doi:10.4278/ajhp.101122-QUAN-387

Bautista, A., Tan, L. S., Ponnusamy, L. D., & Yau, X. (2016). Curriculum integration in arts education: Connecting multiple art forms through the idea of 'space.' *Journal of Curriculum Studies, 48*(5), 610–629. doi:10.1080/00220272.2015.1089940

Beverborg, A. O. G., Sleegers, P. J., Moolenaar, N. M., & van Veen, K. (2020). Fostering sustained teacher learning: A longitudinal assessment of the influence of vision building and goal interdependence on information sharing. *School Effectiveness and School Improvement*. Advance online publication. doi:10.1080/09243453.2020.1754863

Borgatti, S. P., Carley, K. M., & Krackhardt, D. (2006). On the robustness of centrality measures under conditions of imperfect data. *Social Networks, 28*(2), 124–136. doi:10.1016/j.socnet.2005.05.001

Borgatti, S. P., Everett, M. G., & Freeman, L. C. (2002). *Ucinet 6 for Windows: Software for social network analysis.* Analytic Technologies.

Borgatti, S. P., Everett, M. G., & Johnson, J. C. (2018). *Analyzing social networks* (2nd ed.). Sage.

Borgatti, S. P., Everett, M. G., Johnson, J. C., & Agneessens, F. (2022). *Analyzing social networks using R*. Sage Publications.

Bourdieu, P. (1986). The forms of social capital. In J. Richardson (Ed.), *Handbook of theory and research for the sociology of education* (pp. 241–258). Greenwood Press.

Bourdieu, P., & Passeron, J. C. (1977). *Reproduction in education, society and culture*. Sage.

Brown, C., Daly, A. J., & Liou, Y.-H. (2016). Improving trust, improving schools: Findings from a social network analysis of 43 primary schools in England. *Journal of Professional Capital and Community*, *1*(1), 69–91. doi:10.1108/JPCC-09-2015-0004

Brown, C., & Poortman, C. L. (2017). *Networks for learning: Effective collaboration for teacher, school and system improvement*. Routledge. doi:10.4324/9781315276649

Brown, C., Zhang, D., Xu, N., & Corbett, S. (2018). Exploring the impact of social relationships on teachers' use of research: A regression analysis of 389 teachers in England. *International Journal of Educational Research*, *89*, 36–46. doi:10.1016/j.ijer.2018.04.003

Bruner, J. S. (1961). The act of discovery. *Harvard Educational Review*, *31*, 21–32.

Bryk, A. S., & Schneider, B. (2002). *Trust in schools: A core resource for improvement*. Russell Sage Foundation.

Buller, D. B., Morrill, C., Taren, D., Aickin, M., Sennott-Miller, L., Buller, M. K., … Wentzel, T. M. (1999). Randomized trial testing the effect of peer education at increasing fruit and vegetable intake. *JNCI: Journal of the National Cancer Institute*, *91*(17), 1491–1500. doi:10.1093/jnci/91.17.1491

Cann, R. F., Sinnema, C., Daly, A. J., Rodway, J., & Liou, Y.-H. (2022). The power of school conditions: Individual, relational, and organizational influences on educator wellbeing. *Frontiers in Psychology*, *13*, 775614–775614. doi:10.3389/fpsyg.2022.775614

Caughron, J. J., Ristow, T., & Antes, A. L. (2019). Uncertainty and problem solving: The role of leader information-gathering strategies. In M. D. Mumford & C. A. Higgs (Eds.), *Leader thinking skills: Capacities for contemporary leadership* (pp. 71–97). Routledge.

Christakis, N. A., & Fowler, J. H. (2013). Social contagion theory: Examining dynamic social networks and human behavior. *Statistics in Medicine*, *32*(4), 556–577.

Chua, M., & Edmonds, T. (2017). Conversation and participation architectures: Practices for creating dialogic spaces with engineering students. In 2017 ASEE *annual conference & exposition.*

Claridge, T. (2018). *Functions of social capital – Bonding, bridging, linking.* Retrieved from https://www.socialcapitalresearch.com/wp-content/uploads/2018/11/Functions-of-Social-Capital.pdf

Coburn, C. E., & Russell, J. L. (2008). District policy and teachers' social networks. *Educational Evaluation and Policy Analysis*, *30*(3), 203–235. doi:10.3102/0162373708321829

Cohen, D. K., & Mehta, J. D. (2017). Why reform sometimes succeeds: Understanding the conditions that produce reforms that last. *American Educational Research Journal*, *54*(4), 644–690.

Coleman, J. S. (1988). Social capital in the creation of human capital. *American Journal of Sociology*, *94*, S95–S120.

Coleman, J. S. (1997). Social capital in the creation of human capital. In A. H. Halsey, H. Lauder, P. Brown, &

A. Stuart Wells (Eds.), *Education culture, economy and society* (pp. 80–95). Oxford University Press.

Coryn, C. L., Noakes, L. A., Westine, C. D., & Schröter, D. C. (2011). A systematic review of theory-driven evaluation practice from 1990 to 2009. *American Journal of Evaluation*, 32(2), 199–226. doi:10.1177/1098214010389321

Cross, R., Borgatti, S. P., & Parker, A. (2001). Beyond answers: Dimensions of the advice network. *Social Networks*, 23(3), 215–235.

Cross, R., Borgatti, S. P., & Parker, A. (2002). Making the invisible visible: Using social network analysis to support strategic collaboration. *California Management Review*, 44(2), 25–46.

Cummings, S., Bridgman, T., & Brown, K. G. (2016). Unfreezing change as three steps: Rethinking Kurt Lewin's legacy for change management. *Human Relations*, 69(1), 33–60. doi:10.1177/0018726715577707

Daly, A. J. (Ed.). (2010). *Social network theory and educational change*. Harvard Education Press.

Daly, A. J., & Finnigan, K. S. (2011). The ebb and flow of social network ties between district leaders under high-stakes accountability. *American Educational Research Journal*, 48(1), 39–79. doi:10.3102/0002831210368990

Daly, A. J., Liou, Y. H., & Der-Martirosian, C. (2020). A capital idea: Exploring the relationship between human and social capital and student achievement in schools. *Journal of Professional Capital and Community*, 6(1), 7–28. doi:10.1108/JPCC-10-2020-0082

Daly, A. J., Moolenaar, N. M., Der-Martirosian, C., & Liou, Y.-H. (2014). Accessing capital resources: Investigating the effects of teacher human and social capital on student achievement. *Teachers College Record, 116*(7), 1–42.

Damoah, B., & Adu, E. (2019). Challenges teachers face in the integration of Environmental Education into the South African curriculum. *American Journal of Humanities and Social Science Research, 3*(10), 157–166.

Davies, R. (2018). Representing theories of change: Technical challenges with evaluation consequences. *Journal of Development Effectiveness, 10*(4), 438–461. doi:10.1080/19439342.2018.1526202

De Brún, A., & McAuliffe, E. (2018). Social network analysis as a methodological approach to explore health systems: A case study exploring support among senior managers/executives in a hospital network. *International Journal of Environmental Research and Public Health, 15*(3), 511. doi:10.3390/ijerph15030511

de Jong, K. J., Moolenaar, N. M., Osagie, E., & Phielix, C. (2016). Valuable connections: A social capital perspective on teachers' social networks, commitment and self-efficacy. *Pedagogia Social, 28*, 71–83.

DeLay, D., Zhang, L., Hanish, L. D., Miller, C. F., Fabes, R. A., Martin, C. L., ... Updegraff, K. A. (2016). Peer influence on academic performance: A social network analysis of social-emotional intervention effects. *Prevention Science, 17*(8), 903–913. doi:10.1007/s11121-016-0678-8

Donaldson, G. (2015). *Successful futures: Independent review of curriculum and assessment arrangements in Wales*. Retrieved from https://www.gov.wales/sites/default/files/publications/2018-03/successful-futures.pdf

Earp, J. A., Eng, E., O'Malley, M. S., Altpeter, M., Rauscher, G., Mayne, L., … Qaqish, B. (2002). Increasing use of mammography among older, rural African American women: Results from a community trial. *American Journal of Public Health*, 92(4), 646–654.

Education Council of Aotearoa New Zealand. (2018). *Educational leadership capability framework*. Education Council of Aotearoa New Zealand. Retrieved from https://educationcouncil.org.nz/sites/default/files/Leadership_Capability_Framework.pdf

Egan, K. (1998). *Teaching as storytelling*. Routledge.

Ensor, T. M., Bancroft, T. D., & Hockley, W. E. (2019). Listening to the picture-superiority effect: Evidence for the conceptual-distinctiveness account of picture superiority in recognition. *Experimental Psychology*, 66(2), 134–153. doi:10.1027/1618-3169/a000437

Erss, M. (2018). "Complete freedom to choose within limits'—Teachers" views of curricular autonomy, agency and control in Estonia, Finland and Germany. *The Curriculum Journal*, 29(2), 238–256. doi:10.1080/09585176.2018.1445514

Farley-Ripple, E., & Buttram, J. (2015). The development of capacity for data use: The role of teacher networks in an elementary school. *Teachers College Record*, 117(4), 1.

Festinger, L. (1957). *A theory of cognitive dissonance*. Row, Peterson.

Field, J. (2017). *Social capital: The genesis of a concept* (3rd ed.). Routledge. https://www.routledge.com/Social-Capital/Field/p/book/9780415703437

Fowler, J. H., & Christakis, N. A. (2008). Dynamic spread of happiness in a large social network: Longitudinal analysis over 20 years in the Framingham Heart Study. *BMJ: British Medical Journal, 337.*

Frank, K. A., Zhao, Y., Penuel, W. R., Ellefson, N., & Porter, S. (2011). Focus, fiddle, and friends: Experiences that transform knowledge for the implementation of innovations. *Sociology of Education, 84*(2), 137–156.

Friedman, V. J. (2011). Revisiting social space: Relational thinking about organizational change. In A. B. Shani, R. W. Woodman, & W. A. Pasmore (Eds.), *Research in organizational change and development* (Vol. 19, pp. 233–257). Emerald Group. doi:10.1108/S0897-3016(2011)0000019010

Friedman, V., & Putnam, R. (2014). Action science. In D. Coghlan & M. Brydon-Miller (Eds.), *The Sage encyclopedia of action research* (Vols. 1–2). SAGE Publications.

Funnell, S. C., & Rogers, P. J. (2011). *Purposeful program theory: Effective use of theories of change and logic models.* John Wiley & Sons.

Gagné, R. M., & Brown, L. T. (1961). Some factors in the programming of conceptual learning. *Journal of Experimental Psychology, 62*(4), 313–321.

Gaubatz, J. A., & Ensminger, D. C. (2017). Department chairs as change agents: Leading change in resistant environments. *Educational Management Administration & Leadership, 45*(1), 141–163. doi:10.1177/1741143215587307

Gillispie, J., & Chrispeels, J. H. (2008). Us and them: Conflict, collaboration, and the discursive negotiation of multishareholder roles in school district reform. *Small Group Research, 39*(4), 397–437. doi:10.1177/1046496408319877

Goddard, Y. L., Goddard, R. D., & Tschannen-Moran, M. (2007). A theoretical and empirical investigation of teacher collaboration for school improvement and student achievement in public elementary schools. *Teachers College Record*, *109*(4), 877–896.

Gotsis, M., Wang, H., Spruijt-Metz, D., Jordan-Marsh, M., & Valente, T. W. (2013). Wellness partners: Design and evaluation of a web-based physical activity diary with social gaming features for adults. *JMIR Research Protocols*, *2*(1). doi:10.2196/resprot.2132

Granovetter, M. S. (1973). The strength of weak ties. *The American Journal of Sociology*, *78*(6), 1360–1380. doi:10.1086/225469

Granovetter, M. S. (1983). The strength of weak ties: A network theory revisited. *Sociological Theory*, *1*, 201–233. doi:doi:10.2307/202051

Großmann, N., & Wilde, M. (2019). Experimentation in biology lessons: Guided discovery through incremental scaffolds. *International Journal of Science Education*, *41*(6), 759–781. doi:10.1080/09500693.2019.1579392

Guskey, T. R. (2002). Does it make a difference? *Educational Leadership*, *59*(6), 45.

Halbesleben, J. R. B., Novicevic, M. M., Harvey, M. G., & Buckley, M. R. (2003). Awareness of temporal complexity in leadership of creativity and innovation: A competency-based model. *The Leadership Quarterly*, *14*(4), 433–454. doi:10.1016/S1048-9843(03)00046-8

Hannah, D., Sinnema, C., & Robinson, V. (2018). Theory of action accounts of problem-solving: How a Japanese school communicates student incidents to parents. *Management in Education*, *33*(2), 62–69. doi:10.1177/0892020618783809

Hannah, D., Sinnema, C., & Robinson, V. (2021). Understanding curricula as theories of action. *The Curriculum Journal*. doi:10.1002/curj.138

Hanneman, R. A., & Riddle, M. (2005). *Introduction to social network methods*. University of California Riverside.

Hatala, J.-P., & Lutta, J. G. (2009). Managing information sharing within an organizational setting: A social network perspective. *Performance Improvement Quarterly*, *21*(4), 5–33.

Helgason, T., Daniell, T. J., Husband, R., Fitter, A. H., & Young, J. P. W. (1998). Ploughing up the wood-wide web? *Nature*, *394*(6692), 6692. doi:10.1038/28764

Hill, H. (2001). Policy is not enough: Language and the interpretation of state standards. *American Educational Research Journal*, *38*(2), 289–318.

Hopkins, M., Ozimek, D., & Sweet, T. M. (2017). Mathematics coaching and instructional reform: Individual and collective change. *Journal of Mathematical Behavior*, *46*, 215–230.

Hopkins, M., & Spillane, J. P. (2014). Schoolhouse teacher educators: Structuring beginning teachers' opportunities to learn about instruction. *Journal of Teacher Education*, *65*(4), 327–339. doi:10.1177/0022487114534483

Hughes, S., & Lewis, H. (2020). Tensions in current curriculum reform and the development of teachers' professional autonomy. *Curriculum Journal*, *31*(2), 290–302. doi:10.1002/curj.25

Hunter, R. F., de la Haye, K., Murray, J. M., Badham, J., Valente, T. W., Clarke, M., & Kee, F. (2019). Social network interventions for health behaviours and outcomes: A systematic review and meta-analysis. *PLOS Medicine*, *16*(9), 9. doi:10.1371/journal.pmed.1002890

Jordan, J., Shah, K., Phillips, A. W., Hartman, N., Love, J., & Gottlieb, M. (2019). Use of the "step-back" method for education research consultation at the national level: A pilot study. *AEM Education and Training*, *3*(4), 347–352. doi:10.1002/aet2.10349

Kirkpatrick, D., & Kirkpatrick, J. (2006). *Evaluating training programs: The four levels*. Berrett-Koehler Publishers.

Kneen, J., Breeze, T., Davies-Barnes, S., John, V., & Thayer, E. (2020). Curriculum integration: The challenges for primary and secondary schools in developing a new curriculum in the expressive arts. *Curriculum Journal*, *31*(2), 258–275. doi:10.1002/curj.34

Korthagen, F. (2001). An essay review of "Developing Teachers, the Challenges of Lifelong Learning" by Christopher Day; Falmer Press, London/Philadelphia, Educational Change and Development Series (1999). *Teaching and Teacher Education*, *17*(2), 263–269.

Kossinets, G. (2006). Effects of missing data in social networks. *Social Networks*, *28*(3), 247–268. doi:10.1016/j.socnet.2005.07.002

Lakon, C. M., Pechmann, C., Wang, C., Pan, L., Delucchi, K., & Prochaska, J. J. (2016). Mapping engagement in Twitter-based support networks for adult smoking cessation. *American Journal of Public Health*, *106*(8), 1374–1380.

Leana, C. R., & Pil, F. K. (2006). Social capital and organizational performance: Evidence from urban public schools. *Organization Science*, *17*(3), 353–366.

Leat, D., & Thomas, U. (2018). Exploring the role of 'brokers' in developing a localised curriculum. *The Curriculum Journal*, *29*(2), 201–218. doi:10.1080/09585176.2018.1445513

Lewin, K. (1947). Group decision and social change. In T. N. Newcomb & E. L. Hartley (Eds.), *Readings in social psychology* (Vol. 3, pp. 330–344). Henry Holt.

Lin, N. (1999). Building a network theory of social capital. *Connections*, 22(1), 28–51.

Lin, N. (2001). *Social capital: A theory of social structure and action*. Cambridge University Press.

Liou, Y.-H., & Daly, A. J. (2018a). Broken bridges: A social network perspective on urban high school leadership. *Journal of Educational Administration*, 56(5), 562–584. doi:10.1108/JEA-01-2018-0010

Liou, Y.-H., & Daly, A. J. (2018b). Evolving relationships of pre-service teachers: A cohort-based model for growing instructional practice through networks. In S. A. Yoon & K. J. Baker-Doyle (Eds.), *Networked by design* (pp. 85–110). Routledge.

Litt, M. D., Kadden, R. M., Kabela-Cormier, E., & Petry, N. (2007). Changing network support for drinking: Initial findings from the network support project. *Journal of Consulting and Clinical Psychology*, 75(4), 542.

Lortie, D. (1975). *Schoolteacher: A sociological study*. University of Chicago Press.

Luke, D. A., & Harris, J. K. (2007). Network analysis in public health: History, methods, and applications. *Annual Review of Public Health*, 28, 69.

Majolo, B., Schino, G., & Aureli, F. (2012). The relative prevalence of direct, indirect and generalized reciprocity in macaque grooming exchanges. *Animal Behaviour*, 83(3), 763–771. doi:10.1016/j.anbehav.2011.12.026

Mayer, R. E. (2004). Should there be a three-strikes rule against pure discovery learning? The case for guided methods of instruction. *The American Psychologist, 59*(1), 14–19. doi:10.1037/0003-066X.59.1.14

Mayne, J. (2015). Useful theory of change models. *Canadian Journal of Program Evaluation, 30*(2), Article 2. https://journalhosting.ucalgary.ca/index.php/cjpe/article/view/31062

Mayne, J. (2017). Theory of change analysis: Building robust theories of change—The University of Auckland. *Canadian Journal of Program Evaluation, 32*(2), 155–173.

McBride, D. M., & Dosher, B. A. (2002). A comparison of conscious and automatic memory processes for picture and word stimuli: A process dissociation analysis. *Consciousness and Cognition, 11*(3), 423–460. doi:10.1016/S1053-8100(02)00007-7

Mikser, R., Kärner, A., & Krull, E. (2016). Enhancing teachers' curriculum ownership via teacher engagement in state-based curriculum-making: The Estonian case. *Journal of Curriculum Studies, 48*(6), 833–855. doi:10.1080/00220272.2016.1186742

Mills, J., & Harmon-Jones, E. (1999). *Cognitive dissonance: Progress on a pivotal theory in social psychology*. American Psychological Association.

Ministry of Education. (2007). *The New Zealand curriculum*.

Ministry of Education. (2014). *Investing in educational success… Communities of schools guide for schools and kura*. Retrieved from https://www.mcsbot.com/uploads/2/8/1/8/28189425/communities-of-schools-eoi-guide.pdf

Moolenaar, N. M., Daly, A. J., Cornelissen, F., Liou, Y.-H., Caillier, S., Riordan, R., … Cohen, N. A. (2014). Linked to innovation: Shaping an innovative climate through network intentionality and educators' social network position. *Journal of Educational Change, 15*(2), 99–123. doi:10.1007/s10833-014-9230-4

Moolenaar, N., Daly, A., & Sleegers, P. (2011). Ties with potential: Social network structure and innovative climate in Dutch schools. *Teachers College Record, 113*(9), 1983–2017. Education Database.

Moolenaar, N. M., Sleegers, P. J. C., & Daly, A. J. (2012). Teaming up: Linking collaboration networks, collective efficacy, and student achievement. *Teaching and Teacher Education, 28*(2), 251–262. doi:10.1016/j.tate.2011.10.001

Muir, W. M. (2005). Incorporation of competitive effects in forest tree or animal breeding programs. *Genetics, 170*(3), 1247–1259. doi:10.1534/genetics.104.035956

Mumford, M. D., Higgs, C. A., Todd, E. M., & Elliott, S. (Eds.). (2019). Thinking about causes: How leaders identify the critical variables to act on. In M. D. Mumford & C. A. Higgs (Eds.), *Leader thinking skills: Capacities for contemporary leadership* (pp. 122–147). Routledge.

Newton, N. (2020). The rationale for subsidiarity as a principle applied within curriculum reform and its unintended consequences. *The Curriculum Journal, 31*(2), 215–230. doi:10.1002/curj.37

Niemela, M. (2021). Subject matter specific curriculum integration: A quantitative study of Finnish student teachers' integrative content knowledge. *Journal of Education for Teaching, 48*(2), 228–240.

Nijland, F., van Amersfoort, D., Schreurs, B., & de Laat, M. (2018). Stimulating teachers' learning in networks: Awareness, ability, and appreciation. In S. A. Yoon & K. J. Baker-Doyle (Eds.), *Networked by design* (pp. 152–173). Routledge.

O'Connor, S., & Cavanagh, M. (2013). The coaching ripple effect: The effects of developmental coaching on wellbeing across organisational networks. *Psychology of Well-Being: Theory, Research and Practice*, *3*(1), 1–23.

Paivio, A. (1991). Dual coding theory: Retrospect and current status. *Canadian Journal of Psychology*, *45*(3), 255–287.

Paivio, A., & Csapo, K. (1973). Picture superiority in free recall: Imagery or dual coding? *Cognitive Psychology*, *5*(2), 176–206. doi:10.1016/0010-0285(73)90032-7

Patuawa, J., Robinson, V., Sinnema, C., & Zhu, T. (2021). Addressing inequity and underachievement: Middle leaders' effectiveness in problem solving. *Leading and Managing*, *27*(1), 51–78. https://search.informit.org/doi/10.3316/informit.925220205986712

Patulny, R., & Svendsen, G. (2007). Exploring the social capital grid: Bonding, bridging, qualitative, quantitative. *International Journal of Sociology and Social Policy*, *27*, 32–51. doi:10.1108/01443330710722742

Paxton, P. (2002). Social capital and democracy: An interdependent relationship. *American Sociological Review*, *67*(2), 254–277. doi:10.2307/3088895

Peeters, A., & Robinson, V. (2015). A teacher educator learns how to learn from mistakes: Single and double-loop learning for facilitators of in-service teacher education. *Studying Teacher Education*, *11*(3), 213–227. doi:10.1080/17425964.2015.1070728

Peeters, A., Robinson, V., & Rubie-Davies, C. (2020). Theories in use that explain adolescent help seeking and avoidance in mathematics. *Journal of Educational Psychology, 112*(3), 3. doi:10.1037/edu0000423

Pietarinen, J., Pyhältö, K., & Soini, T. (2017). Large-scale curriculum reform in Finland—Exploring the interrelation between implementation strategy, the function of the reform, and curriculum coherence. *The Curriculum Journal, 28*(1), 22–40. doi:10.1080/09585176.2016.1179205

Poortman, C. L., Brown, C., & Schildkamp, K. (2022). Professional learning networks: A conceptual model and research opportunities. *Educational Research, 64*(1), 95–112. doi:10.1080/00131881.2021.1985398

Prell, C. (2012). *Social network analysis: History, theory and methodology*. SAGE.

Putnam, R. D. (1993). *Making democracy work: Civic traditions in modern Italy*. Princeton University Press.

Putnam, R. D. (2000). *Bowling alone: The collapse and revival of American community*. Simon & Schuster.

Putwain, D. W., & von der Embse, N. P. (2019). Teacher self-efficacy moderates the relations between imposed pressure from imposed curriculum changes and teacher stress. *Educational Psychology, 39*(1), 51–64. doi:10.1080/014434 10.2018.1500681

Quintero, E. (2017). *Teaching in context: The social side of education reform*. Harvard Education Press.

Razer, M. (2021). From power struggle to benevolent authority and empathic limit-setting: Creating inclusive school practice with excluded students through action research. *Action Research, 19*(1), 9–36. doi:10.1177/1476750318776730

Reio, T. G., Rocco, T. S., Smith, D. H., & Chang, E. (2017). A critique of Kirkpatrick's evaluation model. *New Horizons*

in Adult Education and Human Resource Development,
29(2), 35–53. doi:10.1002/nha3.20178

Riordan, P. (1995). The philosophy of action science. *Journal
of Managerial Psych*, *10*(6), 6–13. doi:10.1108/
02683949510093821

Robinson, V. (1993). *Problem-based methodology: Research
for the improvement of practice*. Pergamon Press.

Robinson, V. (2001). Embedding leadership in task
performance. In C. W. Evers & K. Wong (Eds.), *Leadership
for quality schooling: International perspectives* (pp. 90–102).
Routledge. doi:10.4324/9780203467237

Robinson, V., & Donald, R. (2014). On the job decision-
making: Understanding and evaluating how leaders solve
problems. In S. Chitpin & C. W. Evers (Eds.), *Decision-
making in educational leadership. Principles, policies, and
practices* (pp. 93–108). Taylor & Francis.

Robinson, V., & Lai, M. (1999). The explanation of practice:
Why Chinese students copy assignments. *International
Journal of Qualitative Studies in Education*, *12*(2), 193–210.
doi:10.1080/095183999236259

Robinson, V., & Lai, M. K. (2005). *Practitioner research for
educators: A guide to improving classrooms and schools*.
Corwin Press.

Robinson, V., Meyer, F., Le Fevre, D., & Sinnema, C. (2020).
The quality of leaders' problem-solving conversations:
Truth-seeking or truth-claiming? *Leadership and Policy in
Schools*, 1–22. doi:10.1080/15700763.2020.1734627

Rogers, P. J., & Weiss, C. H. (2007). Theory-based
evaluation: Reflections ten years on: Theory-based

evaluation: Past, present, and future. *New Directions for Evaluation, 2007*(114), 63–81. doi:10.1002/ev.225

Ronfeldt, M., Farmer, S. O., McQueen, K., & Grissom, J. A. (2015). Teacher collaboration in instructional teams and student achievement. *American Educational Research Journal, 52*(3), 475.

Runco, M. A. (2019). Divergent thinking, creativity and ideation. In J. C. Kaufman & R. J. Sternberg (Eds.), *The Cambridge handbook of creativity* (pp. 413–446). Cambridge University Press.

Scanlan, M., Kim, M., & Ludlow, L. (2019). Affordances and constraints of communities of practice to promote bilingual schooling. *Journal of Professional Capital and Community, 4*(2), 82–106. doi:10.1108/jpcc-01-2018-0003

Schnellert, L. (2020). *Professional learning networks: Facilitating transformation in diverse contexts with equity-seeking communities.* Emerald Publishing Limited. http://ebookcentral.proquest.com/lib/auckland/detail.action?docID=6201153

Schön, D. (1979). Generative metaphor: A perspective on problem-setting in social policy. In A. Ortony (Ed.), *Metaphor and thought* (pp. 254–283). Cambridge University Press.

Schön, D. A. (1993). Generative metaphor a perspective on problem setting in social policy. In A. Ortony (Ed.), *Metaphor and thought* (2nd ed., pp. 137–163). Cambridge University Press.

Schön, D. A. (2017). *The reflective practitioner: How professionals think in action.* Routledge. doi:10.4324/9781315237473

Schwartz, D. L., & Bransford, J. D. (1998). A time for telling. *Cognition and Instruction*, *16*(4), 475–522.

Schwarz, R. M. (2016). *The skilled facilitator: A comprehensive resource for consultants, facilitators, managers, trainers, and coaches* (3rd ed.). John Wiley & Sons.

Scott, J. (2017). *Social network analysis* (4th ed.). Sage Publications.

Sebire, S. J., Jago, R., Banfield, K., Edwards, M. J., Campbell, R., Kipping, R., ... Hollingworth, W. (2018). Results of a feasibility cluster randomised controlled trial of a peer-led school-based intervention to increase the physical activity of adolescent girls (PLAN-A). *The International Journal of Behavioral Nutrition and Physical Activity*, *15*(1). doi:10.1186/s12966-018-0682-4

Shaw, A., DeScioli, P., Barakzai, A., & Kurzban, R. (2017). Whoever is not with me is against me: The costs of neutrality among friends. *Journal of Experimental Social Psychology*, *71*, 96–104. doi:10.1016/j.jesp.2017.03.002

Shelton, R. C., Lee, M., Brotzman, L. E., Crookes, D. M., Jandorf, L., Erwin, D., & Gage-Bouchard, E. A. (2019). Use of social network analysis in the development, dissemination, implementation, and sustainability of health behavior interventions for adults: A systematic review. *Social Science & Medicine*, *220*, 81–101.

Shepard, R. N. (1967). Recognition memory for words, sentences, and pictures. *Journal of Verbal Learning and Verbal Behavior*, *6*(1), 156–163.

Shwartz, Y., Weizman, A., Fortus, D., Krajcik, J., & Reiser, B. (2008). The IQWST experience: Using coherence as a design principle for a middle school science curriculum.

The Elementary School Journal, 109(2), 199–219.
doi:10.1086/590526

Silver, I., & Shaw, A. (2022). When and why "staying out of
it" backfires in moral and political disagreements. *Journal
of Experimental Psychology: General, 151*(10), 2542–2561.
doi:10.1037/xge0001201

Sinnema, C. (2016). The ebb and flow of curricular
autonomy: Balance between local freedom and national
prescription in curricula. In D. Wyse, L. Hayward, &
J. Z. Pandya (Eds.), *The SAGE handbook of curriculum,
pedagogy and assessment* (pp. 965–983). SAGE Publications.

Sinnema, C., & Aitken, G. (2013). Emerging international
trends in curriculum. In M. Priestley & G. J. Biesta (Eds.),
*Reinventing the curriculum: New trends in curriculum
policy and practice* (pp. 141–164). Bloomsbury Academic.

Sinnema, C., Daly, A. J., Liou, Y.-H., & Rodway, J. (2020).
Exploring the communities of learning policy in New Zealand
using social network analysis: A case study of leadership,
expertise, and networks. *International Journal of Educational
Research, 99*, 101492. doi:10.1016/j.ijer.2019.10.002

Sinnema, C., Hannah, D., Finnerty, A., & Daly, A. J. (2021).
A theory of action account of an across-school collaboration
policy in practice. *Journal of Educational Change, 33*(2), 2.

Sinnema, C., Liou, Y.-H., Daly, A., Cann, R., & Rodway, J.
(2021). When seekers reap rewards and providers pay a
price: The role of relationships and discussion in improving
practice in a community of learning. *Teaching and Teacher
Education, 107*, 103474. doi:10.1016/j.tate.2021.103474

Sinnema, C., Nieveen, N., & Priestley, M. (2020). Successful
futures, successful curriculum: What can Wales learn from

international curriculum reforms? *The Curriculum Journal.*
doi:10.1002/curj.17

Sinnema, C., & Stoll, L. (2020). Learning for and realising
curriculum aspirations through schools as learning
organisations. *European Journal of Education, 55,* 9–23.
doi:10.1111/ejed.12381

Spillane, J. P., Shirrell, M., & Sweet, T. M. (2017). The
elephant in the schoolhouse. *Sociology of Education, 90*(2), 2.
doi:10.1177/0038040717696151

Stein, D., & Valters, C. (2012). *Understanding theory
of change in international development* The Justice and
Security Research Programme and The Asia Foundation.

Strange, J. M., & Mumford, M. D. (2005). The origins of vision:
Effects of reflection, models, and analysis. *The Leadership
Quarterly, 16*(1), 121–148. doi:10.1016/j.leaqua.2004.07.006

Thibodeau, P. H., & Boroditsky, L. (2011). Metaphors we
think with: The role of metaphor in reasoning. *PLoS One,*
6(2), 2. doi:10.1371/journal.pone.0016782

Timperley, H. (2008). *Teacher professional learning and
development* (Vol. 18). International Academy of Education
and International Bureau of Education.

Tubaro, P., Ryan, L., Casilli, A. A., & D'Angelo, A. (2021).
Social network analysis: New ethical approaches through
collective reflexivity. Introduction to the special issue of
Social Networks. *Social Networks, 67,* 1–8. doi:10.1016/
j.socnet.2020.12.001

Valente, T. W. (2010). *Social networks and health models,
methods, and applications.* Oxford University Press.

Valente, T. W. (2012). Network interventions. *Science,*
337(6090), 49–53.

Valente, T. W. (2017). Putting the network in network interventions. *Proceedings of the National Academy of Sciences*, *114*(36), 9500–9501.

Valente, T. W., & Davis, R. L. (1999). Accelerating the diffusion of innovations using opinion leaders. *The Annals of the American Academy of Political and Social Science*, *566*(1), 55–67.

van den Boom-Muilenburg, S. N., Poortman, C. L., Daly, A. J., Schildkamp, K., de Vries, S., Rodway, J., & van Veen, K. (2022). Key actors leading knowledge brokerage for sustainable school improvement with PLCs: Who brokers what? *Teaching and Teacher Education*, *110*, 103577. doi:10.1016/j.tate.2021.103577

Van Waes, S., De Maeyer, S., Moolenaar, N. M., Van Petegem, P., & Van den Bossche, P. (2018). Strengthening networks: A social network intervention among higher education teachers. *Learning and Instruction*, *53*, 34–49.

Ward, T. B., & Sifonis, C. M. (1997). Task demands and generative thinking: What changes and what remains the same? *The Journal of Creative Behavior*, *31*(4), 245–259. doi:10.1002/j.2162-6057.1997.tb00797.x

Ward, T. B., Smith, S. M., & Vaid, J. (1997). Conceptual structures and processes in creative thought. In T. B. Ward, S. M. Smith, & J. Vaid (Eds.), *Creative thought: An investigation of conceptual structures and processes* (pp. 1–27). American Psychological Association. doi:10.1037/10227-001

Wasserman, S. (1994). *Social network analysis: Methods and applications*. Cambridge University Press.

Weick, K. E. (1995). *Sensemaking in organizations*. Sage.

Whitehouse, A. J., Maybery, M. T., & Durkin, K. (2006). The development of the picture-superiority effect. *British*

Journal of Developmental Psychology, 24(4), 767–773. doi:10.1348/026151005X74153

Wood, B. (2021). Contours of contested curriculum | Teachers and Curriculum. *Teachers and Curriculum, 21*(1), 55–58.

Woodland, R. H., Barry, S., & Roohr, K. C. (2014). Using social network analysis to promote schoolwide instructional innovation: A case study. *Journal of School Leadership, 24*(1), 114–145.

Woodland, R. H., Douglas, J., & Matuszczak, D. (2021). Assessing organizational capacity for diffusion: A school-based social network analysis case study. *Evaluation and Program Planning, 89*, 101995.

Woolley, A. W., Chabris, C. F., Pentland, A., Hashmi, N., & Malone, T. W. (2010). Evidence for a collective intelligence factor in the performance of human groups. *Science, 330*(6004), 686–688. doi:10.1126/science.1193147

Yarbrough, D. B., Shula, L. M., Hopson, K., & Caruthers, F. A. (2011). *The program evaluation standards: A guide for evaluators and evaluation users* (3rd ed.). Corwin Press SAGE.

Yoon, S. A. (2018). Mechanisms that couple intentional network rewiring and teacher learning to develop teachers' social capital for implementing computer-supported complex systems curricula. In S. A. Yoon & K. J. Baker-Doyle (Eds.), *Networked by design: Interventions for teachers to develop social capital* (pp. 7–23). Routledge.

Yoon, S. A. (2022). Designing complex systems curricula for high school biology: A decade of work with the BioGraph Project. In O. B. Assaraf & M.-C. Knippels (Eds.), *Fostering understanding of complex systems in biology education* (pp. 227–247). Springer.

Yoon, S. A., & Baker-Doyle, K. J. (Eds.). (2018). *Networked by design: Interventions for teachers to develop social capital*. Routledge.

Yoon, S., Yom, J. K., Yang, Z., & Liu, L. (2017). The effects of teachers' social and human capital on urban science reform initiatives: Considerations for professional development. *Teachers College Record*, *119*(4), 1–32.

Young, G. F., Scardovi, L., Cavagna, A., Giardina, I., & Leonard, N. E. (2013). Starling flock networks manage uncertainty in consensus at low cost. *PLOS Computational Biology*, *9*(1), e1002894. doi:10.1371/journal.pcbi.1002894

Zhao, K., Wang, X., Cha, S., Cohn, A. M., Papandonatos, G. D., Amato, M. S., … Graham, A. L. (2016). A multirelational social network analysis of an online health community for smoking cessation. *Journal of Medical Internet Research*, *18*(8), e5985.

INDEX